'An in-depth examination of how B2B brands can build trusted relationships in today's volatile information environment. Required reading for communicators and marketers across the world, with plenty of invaluable insight from some of the world's top B2B players.'
Arun Sudhaman, CEO and Editor-in-Chief, The Holmes Report

'Many B2B brands today publish more material in a week than *Time* magazine did during its heyday. Yet embarking on brand journalism is fraught with perils and pitfalls. What constitutes a good story? How can compelling content be created not just once, but continually and indefinitely? And how, in the era of fake news, can brands engender and earn the trust of their audiences? This book tells you how, both with practical advice and scores of real world examples. It's a must for the B2B content marketer.'
Rebecca Lieb, analyst and author of *Content: The Atomic Particle of Marketing*

'This book is a comprehensive review of how B2B brands can build the most important aspect of sales and marketing today: trust. It's filled with real-world, applicable examples that can help marketers become a trusted source.'
Robert Rose, Founder, The Content Advisory

'This book provides a fresh look at the role of brand journalism in successful brand building. Rich in examples, frameworks and models, *Powerful B2B Content* provides a very hands-on analysis, exploring the careful balance between creating compelling digital content that actively engages audiences throughout the customer journey and brand positioning that is authentic. A top read for brand experts and business leaders alike.'
Christine Diamente, Head of Brand, Nokia

'The only way to acquire new customers today is through stories that generate trust. In *Powerful B2B Content*, Gay Flashman shows us not just why, but also how to generate trust that leads to new customer relationships and business growth. All business leaders need to pick up a copy of this book today.'
Michael Brenner, CEO, speaker and bestselling author of *Mean People Suck* and *The Content Formula*

'A richly illustrated guide to how businesses can create their own media brands.'
Mark Jones, Head of Digital Content, World Economic Forum

'I was lucky enough to work with and learn from Gay Flashman in the newsroom in the late 1990s. Journalism and marketing have undergone a revolution since then, and Gay has been riding that rollercoaster all along – there is no one better placed to help you take control of your business's narrative, own your story and use it to connect with your customers beyond the level of mere transaction.'
Julian March, CEO, Made by Many

'For many companies in the B2B sphere, the first point of interaction with clients, on a multi-touch point journey, is through content, be it digital or above the line. To entice customers a brand must convey an enduring narrative that resonates with their target industries. This book provides insights from leading industry experts and acts as a guide on the production of powerful content with purpose. It is a must-read for B2B marketers aiming to create engaging content that portrays their client's story.'
Georgia Halston, Founder, Halston Marketing

'In this comprehensive guide, Gay Flashman explains why journalistic thinking, newsroom practices and editorial values underpin successful brand journalism. Easy to say, difficult to do, but here's someone who has walked the walk in some of the world's busiest newsrooms and knows a thing or two about engaging storytelling and how to deliver it. Read and learn.'
Gary Rogers, Editor-in-Chief, RADAR AI

'Storytelling helps B2B brands to cut through the noise and helps in winning the hearts and minds of buyers. Gay Flashman shares her insights on how purpose-driven storytelling can help marketers engage with their audiences and create lasting and meaningful relationships.'
Ashish Babu, CMO (Europe and UK), Tata Consultancy Services

'If content is still going to be king then great storytelling is how we must cut through the noise to deliver that content. But this in itself won't be enough for businesses to win in this complex world. Gay Flashman tells us that building trust and relationships are essential to not only winning but keeping new customers. A great resource for all B2B marketers.'
Howard Krais, President, International Association of Business Communicators (IABC), UK and Ireland

'If you're a brand looking to create a content practice, *Powerful B2B Content* provides a detailed roadmap for setting up shop.'
Melanie Deziel, Founder, StoryFuel

'Every business must be engaging and inspiring if it wants to remain relevant and reach new customers. This handbook is chock full of dos and don'ts from brand journalism leaders shaping the craft. They explain why authentic storytelling is essential for business success, and how to do it right.'
Ken Kaplan, Editorial Director, Nutanix

'A must-read for anyone working in the B2B sector. If you are a business leader, read and be inspired. If you are a communications expert, read and discover best-in-class practices to build your business case. If you're an expert or a beginner in corporate communications, read it and save yourself the headache of starting from scratch. Stories are the fabric of our world. With this text Gay Flashman cracks open the art and science of becoming a master storytelling company.'
Casilda Malagon, global communications professional and Co-Founder, Archetypical

'In this compelling narrative, Gay Flashman practises what she preaches: she awakens our interest, informs us fully and engagingly, and leaves us converted to the critical importance of building and nurturing our brand stories. Vital reading for boards and the C-Suite.'
Piers Cumberlege, Chair, Straightview International

Powerful B2B Content

*Using brand journalism to create compelling
and authentic storytelling*

Gay Flashman

KoganPage

Publisher's note

Every possible effort has been made to ensure that the information contained in this book is accurate at the time of going to press, and the publishers and author cannot accept responsibility for any errors or omissions, however caused. No responsibility for loss or damage occasioned to any person acting, or refraining from action, as a result of the material in this publication can be accepted by the editor, the publisher or the author.

First published in Great Britain and the United States in 2020 by Kogan Page Limited

2nd Floor, 45 Gee Street	122 W 27th St, 10th Floor	4737/23 Ansari Road
London	New York, NY 10001	Daryaganj
EC1V 3RS	USA	New Delhi 110002
United Kingdom		India

www.koganpage.com

© Gay Flashman, 2020

ISBNs

Hardback	978 1 78966 101 9
Paperback	978 1 78966 099 9
Ebook	978 1 78966 100 2

British Library Cataloguing-in-Publication Data

A CIP record for this book is available from the British Library.

Library of Congress Cataloging-in-Publication Data

Names: Flashman, Gay, author.
Title: Powerful B2B content : using brand journalism to create compelling and authentic storytelling / Gay Flashman.
Description: London, United Kingdom ; New York, NY : Kogan Page, 2020. | Includes bibliographical references and index.
Identifiers: LCCN 2019047562 (print) | LCCN 2019047563 (ebook) | ISBN 9781789661019 (hardback) | ISBN 9781789660999 (paperback) | ISBN 9781789661002 (ebook)
Subjects: LCSH: Industrial marketing. | Branding (Marketing) | Storytelling.
Classification: LCC HF5415.1263 .F595 2020 (print) | LCC HF5415.1263 (ebook) | DDC 658.8/04–dc23
LC record available at https://lccn.loc.gov/2019047562
LC ebook record available at https://lccn.loc.gov/2019047563

Typeset by Integra Software Services, Pondicherry
Print production managed by Jellyfish
Printed and bound by CPI Group (UK) Ltd, Croydon, CR0 4YY

For Dad

CONTENTS

12 Bringing your newsroom to life 207

LIST OF FIGURES AND TABLES

TABLES

ABOUT THE AUTHOR

Gay Flashman is a pioneer of brand journalism, blending her experience as a senior journalist, communications professional and digital marketer to create compelling content strategies for some of the world's leading brands.

Gay is the founder of Formative Content, a global content marketing agency that works with clients such as the World Economic Forum, Microsoft, Coca-Cola, Standard Chartered, Mitsubishi Heavy Industries and Tata Consultancy Services, creating powerful B2B content ranging from social media and blog content to thought leadership and white papers.

Starting in newspapers, Gay built a career at the BBC and ITN in TV news journalism, culminating in her position as Managing Editor at Channel 4 News and Channel 5 News. Following a move to Sydney, she worked as a management consultant at both ABC News and SBS in Australia before founding Formative Content.

Gay is a frequent public speaker on topics relating to content, digital marketing and media.

FOREWORD

This is a book about a hidden power: the power of storytelling.

It's not the first thing that comes to mind when you think of marketing. It's not about the hard sell. It's about finding the human stories that pulse beneath the surface of big corporations and that connect all of us, in all of our hopes and dreams and fears. It is about building trust.

Genuinely impactful, disintermediated content lets brands amplify the issues and the topics that matter to them, and talk directly to the people they want to engage with.

That is the power that this book uncovers. Not marketing advertorial, but genuine editorial. At its best, it delivers substance over slogans, and insights over earworms.

I cannot think of a better person to explain the value of story-driven content marketing than Gay Flashman. She has been around content and journalism all her working life, as a journalist, as a television executive, and as a founder and CEO. She's created the strategies to deploy meaningful content and the material to make it real for some of the planet's most progressive businesses.

In *Powerful B2B Content*, Gay Flashman shows how to use content to develop an organizational voice, to give shape and meaning to business issues, to encourage knowledge to slip the bonds of jargon and make the effort to be discoverable, discussable, and shareable.

There are three big changes taking place in this century's workplace. People, young and old, expect more from employers. Yes, they want careers, but they also want causes they can believe in and a community they can belong to. Progress, purpose and values. These are frightening things when you are conditioned to talking to shareholders who want profit, dividend and predictability.

People expect to share their experiences through social media. Not just the experiences of their leisure time either; they also want to share insights and knowledge on professional and personal networks such as LinkedIn or Pinterest. They want to share things their families care about on networks such as Facebook, WeChat or TikTok. Sharing has taken the place of magazines and newspapers, paperback bookshelves and photograph albums in people's online spaces.

People consume media differently. That means the old gatekeepers have lost their power. Remember these forces apply not just to some faceless global audience or valued target demographic, they apply to an organization's people: its staff, its employees, its stakeholders. These are the future advocates and ambassadors of first resort.

If you are not in people's headphones, or on their screens – if you do not have a route into their attention, then where are you?

What Gay lays out in the chapters ahead is how to get there, practically and purposefully. It's a journey that can benefit anyone, from the smallest start-up to the biggest corporate behemoth. You could not have a better guide.

Adrian Monck
Managing Director
The World Economic Forum

ACKNOWLEDGEMENTS

Without the support, contribution and guidance of many people, this book would not have seen the light of day. To all of those who leant their skills, their insight, guidance and support – a heartfelt thank you.

It's been quite a journey from the newsrooms of ITN, the BBC and Sky to running an international content agency, and the experience and knowledge gained in those pressurised, dynamic and utterly stimulating newsrooms has stood me in good stead for the work that was to follow.

To Adrian Monck, thank you for the vision and dogged pursuance of the goal of innovator in brand publishing.

Thanks to my clients, many of whom offered their precious time for interviews, making themselves available and trusting their thoughts to me; many others shared their knowledge through the work we have developed together. Special thanks to Mark Jones, Abhinav Kumar, Ashish Babu, Dan Lochmann, Jim Cox and Laura Price.

To all the marketing thinkers, writers and consultants who gave their time and their enthusiasm, and whose books and blogs I have read over the years, thank you. Special mention to those interviewed for the book, including Mark Schaefer, Melanie Deziel, Lisa Moretti, Michael Brenner, Neal Schaffer, Rebecca Lieb, Rob Blackie, Robert Rose, Amy Hatch, Sarah Goodall, Tom Foremski, Luke Kintigh, Ken Kaplan, Krista Ruhe and Laura Hamlyn.

The expertise I have developed over the last five years has been built on the hard work of a dedicated team at our agency, Formative Content. Ongoing gratitude to the senior leadership team, writers, senior content editors, client services team, web team and operations team busy in our Beaconsfield newsroom. You have all contributed over the last five years to much of the output and insight referenced here.

Alex Weller and the Above Digital team – thank you all for your ongoing support and web smarts. To videographer and editor Mike Sedgwick and PR guru Wendy Richmond – thanks for the fun times, your relentless professionalism and years of friendship.

Thanks to Jenny Volich and the team at Kogan Page.

For the strategic messaging guidance, for all the years of friendship, laughs and ongoing reassurance, a huge thank you to Deborah Turness and Charlotte Hume. Thanks also to Brian, for his unstinting and generous support.

Selina Swift deserves a special mention for being the voice of calm, and a force of positive energy, helping with all referencing, lay-out and outreach for which I had neither the skills, the time, nor the patience. Peter Crush, thank you for the help in knocking some of these words into better shape; years writing TV intros and headlines did not prepare me for the challenge of writing a book.

The path from a business of two people in a room to a team of more than fifty has been in equal measure an eventful and challenging one. Guidance from Neil Backwith, Piers Cumberlege, Damon Clark, Natalie Richer and Brian Harris has been invaluable.

To Paul Muggeridge. I am so grateful that our worlds collided. I could not have asked for a more impressive, dynamic and ridiculously focused partner with whom to have shared this journey. Here's to the future and all it brings.

Sorry to my boys, Joe and Sam, for all those lost evenings and weekends.

And for his unfailing patience, love and support, eternal gratitude to John Wilson.

01

Why use brand journalism as part of your content marketing mix?

The lens through which we view our B2B communications and marketing materials is becoming increasingly blurred. Not only have the last few years witnessed an explosion in the sheer number of channels that didn't exist before, but the amount and complexity of information that these channels contain is reaching almost unfathomable levels.

It's staggering to think that today an extra *2.5 quintillion* bytes of data will be created, and will continue to be created, each and every day. To put this into some sort of perspective, 90 per cent of the data that's ever been created in the history of mankind was created in the last two years.[1]

Unsurprisingly, this explosion of channels means brands – whether they occupy the B2B or B2C space – have an increasingly hard task when it comes to reaching customers and audiences. With the number of stakeholders multiplying and the touchpoints with which they connect also proliferating, buying cycles have become much more complicated. It's no longer enough for brands to start engaging their target audience at the top of the traditional sales journey. What they need now is some sort of 'brand warm-up'. B2B brands must find a way to build a presence before the buyer even reaches the top of the sales funnel. As content marketing expert Robert Rose puts it: 'The remit of marketing these days is to have a very large part of the top of funnel experience/pre-customer phase.'[2]

What does this really mean? What's often forgotten is that selling a product is actually a human-to-human experience; it's about telling stories that resonate about your brand in a broader sense, or which align your brand with a particular way of thinking. It's about creating stories that support marketing efforts even *before* potential buyers start on the journey to purchase. If created well, and in a way that occupies the various networks your audiences engage with, these *journalistic* stories can deliver solid reputational impact.

Making your brand a contender

In other words, success in our multi-channel world is about establishing your brand as a 'contender' – one that consumers will consider, at the point they (or an influencer of a buyer) decide they have a need. Brands must establish themselves in a more considered and strategic way, using editorial content, in the places and spaces audiences are inhabiting – even before they exhibit a product or service need.

Volume of information

Grabbing the attention of any customer, whether B2B or B2C, is growing more challenging every day.

In recent years there has been an almost exponential rise in the number of news and information outlets delivering articles, blogs, so-called news and other forms of content in all its guises. Some of this content originates from traditional or recognized news sources, but a rising proportion is from personal bloggers and previously unknown publishers.

But the quality of much of this output is questionable. Eighty per cent of blog writers do all their writing themselves without any outsourcing for fact checking (according to data from SEO Tribunal[3]). It's well reported that many posts are ill thought out, only loosely researched and often not substantiated, and yet they appear in many people's social feeds and inboxes. Add to this the content that is simply duplicated across outlets, cut and pasted and shared, and it's not difficult to see that there is a wave of mediocre information swamping all of us.

But as well as an ever-growing total volume of information, it is the sheer quantity of outlets and voices competing for our attention that is also reaching staggering proportions.

As the internet has democratized audience reach, there has been massive growth in niche news outlets and sites delivering the 'long tail' of views and positioning – often representing the less mainstream and minority thinking. Some see this as a welcome sign of diversification. But not only do some argue this is a breeding ground for 'fake news', other media commentators are worried about the impact these new sources of information – more often than not from social media sites – are having. Many audiences are now abandoning traditional and trusted news outlets for those that are more often than not echo chambers for their beliefs.

If this wasn't challenging enough, not all content we see (primarily in our social feeds) is even written, generated or shared by humans. Some is being generated in troll farms[4] creating, distributing and sharing content aimed at manipulating political thinking, or undermining fact-based insight in healthcare, or the economy.

The impact of all this cannot be underestimated. We live in a time where some people are veering towards content or phony stories that support their beliefs, while others are being turned off by traditional media. All-told, trust and credibility of news sources has never been so highly questioned. As the Pew Research Centre recently found, the growth in content has been such that only around one in five Americans said they trusted what was shared to them by news organizations, family or friends. Social media was trusted by even fewer. Only 4 per cent of web-using adults said they trusted what they saw and read, no matter who shared it. Audiences are now ever more aware that the information that is delivered to them is biased – almost three-quarters of those surveyed agreed with this.[5]

Legislation limiting marketing

As well as the marketing profession's own efforts to stop people being deluged by too many untargeted messages, governments are also legislating to stop the rising wave of spam and unwanted push engagement.

General Data Protection Regulation (GDPR) rules have applied in the European Union since May 2018, and they limit the way companies can use, share and store data about individuals. Personal data can't be used without the consent of the person concerned, and it can't be forwarded to others or re-used in any way.

While it's challenging to find data on the true impact of GDPR on email marketing and telemarketing, Facebook reported that a temporary fall in user registrations, and a decline in ad revenue in early 2018, was linked to the legislation. Why? More and more consumers now value the importance of privacy. Research has found that almost 70 per cent of US adults aren't comfortable with companies sharing and selling their data and online activity – and more than half of these report taking specific action to limit data collection when they're using apps and websites. Many will even stop using the company altogether if need be.[6]

Against this background, it's perhaps unsurprising that research group Forrester noted that the number of Fortune 100 firms explaining their commitment to consumers' privacy as part of their corporate social responsibility grew from 21 in 2017 to 28 a year later.[7] With the number of GDPR-prompted complaints growing, it's no wonder areas outside Europe – including California, Brazil, Japan and India – are also debating introducing similar regulation.[8]

Buyers doing their own research

In the recent past there were only a limited number of ways vendors could engage with buyers, and much of this engagement was one to one, or face to face. There was also only a limited extent to which buyers could gather information to inform their buying decision. Today, however, B2B buying decisions are characterized and influenced by a variety of factors – and a lot of these take place before customers even contact a company to find out about a product. The decision about whether to engage with a brand and purchase its products might start and finish completely at the online research stage – research shows that almost half of all B2B buyers will touch or engage with three to five pieces of content before they contact a salesperson.[9]

In fact, the business consumer is now so digitally sophisticated, that according to Lori Wizdo at Forrester Research:[10]

- more than two-thirds (68 per cent) of B2B buyers say they prefer to research on their own, and online;
- 62 per cent of B2B buyers say they now develop their selection criteria or finalize a vendor shortlist based solely on digital content;
- some 60 per cent of B2B buyers prefer not to contact a sales rep as the primary source of information.

The message here couldn't be clearer: brands that don't have the right type of digital content – that is content which is engaging and appealing to decision makers – have lost their sale before it's even begun.

A crisis of trust

B2B brands that have managed to 'cut through the noise', get their audience's attention and get themselves noticed still don't have an easy ride of it. As I have already indicated, trust is the last big dominant issue. Build trust, and relationships are forged and fostered. As we know, though, audiences don't appreciate push messages; they want to feel an affinity with the brands that they are dealing with.

Accenture puts it neatly in one of its recent research reports:

> The heightened transparency inherent in our digital world means trust is a highly flammable, ever-present concern... companies need to very intentionally create a culture of building, maintaining and preserving trust, and bake it into their DNA, strategy and day-to-day operations.[11]

Trust is important because it impacts your buyers, your investors, your partners and your employees. It's not only important to reinforce and measure, but also to communicate to your stakeholders and audiences. Failure of trust is more pervasive in young people in

Western societies, according to research by Deloitte.[12] In fact, optimism is at an all-time low amongst young people. Overall, millennials are less trusting across the board – whether it's of religious leaders, politicians or the mainstream media. Millennials and Gen Zs are more likely to patronize and support companies who share their own values.

The good news is that emerging research indicates buyers are more ready to accept that vendor content is trustworthy.[13] Better vendor trust is creating what Forrester's Laura Ramos calls a 'B2B content arms race', with B2B firms 'trying to achieve competitive advantage by producing any possible content that any possible buyer could possibly need at any possible time.'[14]

However, before looking at this in more detail, it's worth examining just how trust levels currently differ across channels.

Challenges to mainstream media

Trust in traditional media, and all media generally, has declined, but there is a growing 'trust gap' between broadcast and new media. According to the YouGov-Cambridge Globalism Project, Britons in 2019 are the least trusting of social media, out of people in 22 nations including France, Germany and the United States.[15] It found just 12 per cent trusted information from social media, while 83 per cent had little or no trust in platforms such as Facebook and Twitter. Just two sources of information were trusted by a majority of Britons: national TV news channels (61 per cent) and local news organizations (54 per cent).

While traditional news brands (NBC, ABC, the BBC), have seen the new kids on the block (BuzzFeed, NowThis and the like) telling stories that capture young people's attention in much more engaging ways, there's still confusion between what is fake and what isn't. This hasn't been helped by the failure of social media platforms themselves – which have been widely condemned for helping to propagate much of the fake news.

The corrosive influence of fake news is such that Edelman's Trust Barometer 2019 found that while there has been a rise in people consuming news, more than 70 per cent worry about fake news or false information being 'used as a weapon'.[16] The net result is that audiences – being fed a diet of trash from all sides and from all channels – often struggle to discern fact from fiction.

Advertising concerns

In parallel with confusion about what parts of the news we should believe in, is the very real concern that exists about the integrity of the advertising industry as a whole. Even though trust in advertising has been falling for the last few decades, more recently trust has been melting at an accelerating pace, with consumer 'belief' in the sector now at a record low (of 25 per cent). It is, so research says, due to the huge volume of ads, their repetition, their obtrusiveness and irrelevance.[17]

As Lord Puttnam, one of the greats of the UK media industry, recently put it:

> Every one of us has a colossal job on our hands in the process
> of recreating trust – not in the system, which in many ways has
> only discredited itself, but in some kind of a system which we feel
> comfortable to gather around and support. Building trust is a human
> activity, and is very unlikely to be achieved solely through the use of
> analytics and algorithms. Simply looked at from the fairly narrow
> perspective of advertising – our role is all about building 'trust' – trust
> in brands, trust in our message, trust in each other.[18]

> Society wants new spokespeople.

It's not just the media and the advertising industries that are struggling to maintain trust in the eyes of outsiders and of audiences. Perhaps top of the list in many Western countries is the demise in respect for politicians. Democratic governments around the world are now mistrusted more than ever before, by as much as 80 per cent in some countries, according to the Edelman Trust Barometer. Whether it's from the handling of Brexit in the UK, to the rise of conflict and confrontation politics in the United States, or the emergence of populist groups such as yellow vests (*les gilets jaunes*) in France, there's been a shift in deference that has seen politicians lose much of the respect they had in the post-war era.

The opportunity: brand purpose

With threat arguably comes opportunity. The trust vacuum left by media, advertising, politicians, and by falling respect for the broader establishment opens up opportunities for senior business leaders and thinkers to demonstrate their credentials through sensible, considered thought leadership.

Organizations have earned their right to step into that space, to talk about the areas that they know and understand. They can do this safe in the knowledge audiences can filter and curate their own narratives – which (in an ideal world) are taken from a range of sources rather than an echo chamber of their own making.

In our interview, Founder and Chief Strategy Officer of The Content Advisory, Robert Rose, described the importance of earning not only our audience's attention but also its trust.

> Attention is not hard to get. You can get attention. You can buy attention. But that attention is fleeting. It's easy to grab somebody's attention for 10 seconds. All you have to do is be controversial or pay for it, and you can get something in front of someone to get their attention. But it's holding that attention that's the hard part; it's holding it for any length of time and deepening the trust so that they want to do things that favour you. That is the difficult part.
>
> That's where the power of content marketing truly comes in, by delivering value before you've even asked for anything, in other words, before you've asked for their name, or their registration, or their email address, or any kind of transaction. You're treating them as if they were a customer already. You're treating them as if they were a valuable relationship to you by delivering value without them even asking for it. And that, to me, makes all the other elements of trust easier.

Your brand conversations should reflect:

- **Honesty** – ensure any stories you develop on behalf of your company exhibit honesty and clarity on the thoughts, views and opinions of the organization.
- **Connection** – build case studies and human examples from within your organization to develop empathy and build relationships.
- **Value** – offer insight that taps into the needs of the customer.
- **Reliability** – don't start the conversation unless you can maintain it.

The power of thoughtfully told stories

It's not just employers and audiences who believe in the power of thought leadership. Employees also believe more than ever that their organization should take the lead on change in the broader environment and the world around them. According to Edelman's Trust Barometer, in 2019 more than 70 per cent felt that a company ought to act in a way that enables it to both increase profits and improve economic and social conditions in the markets in which it operates.[19]

So, what better way to demonstrate you are doing than through your own thoughtfully told stories? Telling your audience what you believe in (and why) should today be considered a vital part of your brand-building strategy. As David Roman explains below, flogging products no longer works. Today there's an expectation brands will share the same beliefs as their consumers – and this is equally relevant in B2B. With data showing that more than half of consumers will boycott brands that don't share their beliefs, there's no reason why this shouldn't be true of the B2B space too.[20] It's B2B brands especially that have seen the customer journey evolve and become more complex with a proliferation of touchpoints, platforms and even the number of people involved in a sale/purchase.

CASE STUDY

Lenovo takes the brand beyond tech innovation

'Now we have become a $50 billion company, Lenovo has to be tighter in terms of what we stand for and what we represent', said David Roman, senior VP and CMO of Lenovo, recently interviewed in the *Drum*. 'When you look at people buying technology today, especially millennials, they expect to have a relationship with the brand. They expect to know about the company. They want the company to share their values. There's a broader set of things than just the technology itself, especially now as we move into cloud-based solutions. There's an expectation of trust and how the company is going to maintain privacy and security.'[21]

The complex path to a sale

It was in 1898 that travelling salesman Elias St Elmo Lewis first coined his famous 'journey to sale' concept – neatly summarized by his AIDA acronym (Awareness, Interest, Desire and Action).

To this day, the basic premise behind what creates sales largely remains unchanged. It could also be argued the sales funnel he first described differs little – it simply has more outlets, touchpoints and platforms through which customers can be engaged. As marketing commentator, professor and strategist Mark Ritson writes:

> The sales funnel precedes the invention of television, direct mail, telemarketing, cinema ads, the internet and smartphones. Each and every one of these technologies has changed the tactical options available to marketers, but the essential challenge of marketing strategy and the enduring value of a properly derived sales funnel remain undimmed.[22]

The rise of digital communications means there are even more touchpoints along the customer journey, and each of those might be delivered on a different platform. According to McKinsey, 'the average B2B customer now uses six different channels over the course of their decision-making journey'.[23] The new challenge is complexity of engagement. And it's this complexity of engagement at different stages of the buyer journey that sits against the backdrop of increased complexity of communication and a growing mistrust in our traditional media, advertising and marketing. As marketing guru Seth Godin writes:

> … the newly empowered consumer has discovered that what looks like clutter to the marketer feels like choice. They've come to realize that there are an infinite number of choices, an endless parade of alternatives. For the marketer, it's like trying to sell sand in a desert.[24]

Without a profile or some sort of digital relationship, organizations wanting to be included in the procurement process can lose a sale before any formal Request for Proposal (RFP) process has even been started. As a McKinsey & Co report concluded, when getting attention becomes harder, it's all the more important to build brand awareness and engagement:

> Faced with a plethora of choices and communications, consumers tend to fall back on the limited set of brands that have made it through the wilderness of messages. Brand awareness matters: brands in the initial consideration set can be up to three times more likely to be purchased eventually than brands that aren't in it.[25]

Key to success is to 'interrupt' the decision-making process with your brand message in as appealing a way as possible. If you can push through the noise – be clever with your messaging, not just shout the loudest – there is scope for brands to use storytelling and brand journalism to gain awareness and start the journey to a trust position. Marketing expert and author Michael Brenner explains in an interview for this book that the issue is not that audiences don't want content, it's that they are not served the content that they need:

> Research shows that buyers are actually quite open and are looking for more content from brands that is educational. I don't think audiences are completely jaded. They are, increasingly, open to brands providing expert-level thought leadership or brand journalism (whatever your preferred term) – they are just disappointed at how few brands are providing it.

The issue is that the natural instinct of the business is to promote itself – this is true in marketing, with the C-suite, and it's certainly true for sales teams. Everybody thinks that their job is to talk about how great their products are and how great the company is. In plain terms, it's the desire to promote that gets in the way.

Finding ways to connect

If storytelling and brand journalism is the answer, the challenge for companies using it is how to connect with their audiences in this fragmented environment. How do organizations cut through with their messaging and engage audiences? How can connections with B2B buyers be made within an ever more complex, emotional and extending sales journey?

Adrian Monck is Managing Director at the World Economic Forum. Interviewed about the Forum's approach to publishing, he explained his belief that an organization could drive its own coverage by disintermediating traditional media:

> We took as our starting point the idea that an organization could use stories to tell the world more about its own mission and its own passion and its own concerns, and then bring that same storytelling approach to people in its organization and in its stakeholder group. The people you engage with, the people you work with, all of those are your audiences as well as the world at large, and telling stories is the most powerful way we know to touch people.

> How do you bring that approach to your own organization or your own business with authenticity and integrity? In my case, the path went from being a professor and thinking about journalism, to realizing that organizations could also embrace some of the values of journalism and be part of the future of what journalism is becoming.

> One of the most important things for any organization, any journalism organization, is having those values – editorial integrity and telling stories respectfully. To do that you have to recognize your organization's

boundaries, in terms of its ability to speak to issues, and you have to make sure that within those boundaries it can communicate with integrity and with authenticity.

The rise of brand purpose

Brands are increasingly expected to stand up for what they believe, and tell stories that align to those beliefs, to demonstrate their brand purpose more pervasively than ever before.

Bill Theofilou, a senior managing director in Accenture Strategy, puts it this way: 'A brand must solve a problem or meet a need. How well it does that, and how well it creates loyalty, affinity and connections with its customers determines the winners from the losers.'[26]

Accenture's own research refers to the 'rise of the purpose-led brand' – stating that its survey of more than 2,000 US consumers found that more than 60 per cent want companies to take a stand on broadly relevant issues such as transparency, fair employment and sustainability. They want to do business with companies that broadly align with their own values.

FIGURE 1.1   Finding the content sweet spot

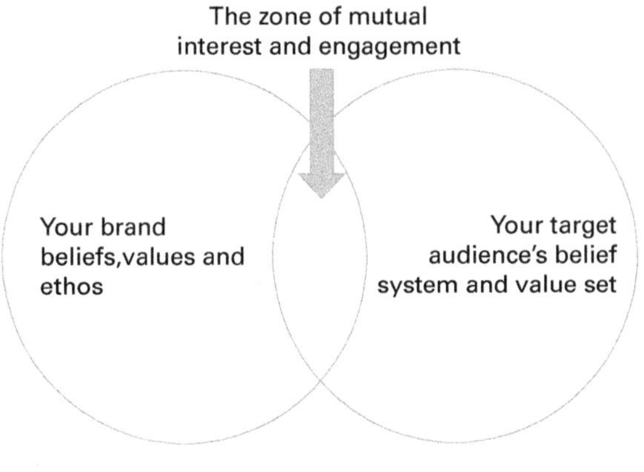

The zone of mutual
interest and engagement

Your brand
beliefs, values and
ethos

Your target
audience's belief
system and value set

Finding your purpose

According to research commissioned by Waggoner Edstrom and Quartz, the need for businesses to have true and authentic purpose is now 'table stakes' and there is an 'inextricable link between social issues and business strategy'. It adds: 'Companies can no longer operate in a vacuum. As 84 per cent of our respondents say, customers will demand greater transparency and assurance that the brands they support have a positive impact on society.'[27]

You don't need to go far to find those that are really embracing this. Multinational consumer goods company Unilever has shaped its brand in recent years with purpose at the heart of its offer. The company has even created a website and mission to support others to do the same thing, called Selling with Purpose.[28]

But this isn't the full extent to which communicating purpose now goes. Brands and business are now expected to have strong views (and associated action) on social issues such as the environment, equality and politics. Satya Nadella (CEO, Microsoft), Marc Benioff (CEO, Salesforce), and Anne Boden (CEO, Starling Bank, behind its #makemoneyequal campaign), are some of the leading exponents of this.

The new challenge for companies might be ascertaining just how comfortable they are straying into potentially tricky, but also potentially beneficial areas. However, in his annual Letter to Investors entitled *Purpose and Profit*,[29] Larry Fink, chairman and CEO of BlackRock, was unambiguous:

> Unnerved by fundamental economic changes and the failure of government to provide lasting solutions, society is increasingly looking to companies, both public and private, to address pressing social and economic issues. These issues range from protecting the environment to retirement to gender and racial inequality, among others. Purpose is not a mere tagline or marketing campaign; it is a company's fundamental reason for being – what it does every day to create value for its stakeholders. Purpose is not the sole pursuit of profits but the animating force for achieving them.

Brand purpose driving value

At a time where trust in news brands is reduced, what Fink *et al* are saying is simple. Why not turn to corporates and established specialist brands – alongside other, traditional outlets and news sources – for information and insight?

Often procurement teams will want to understand commitment to targets around equality, gender balance, access, supply chain viability and commercial approach, whilst governments are legislating changes and approaches to how businesses work. Increasingly there is a focus on sustainable and ethical procurement and standards. Integrating these narratives into your public-facing assets – website, blog site, social media channels – is just one key part of building reputation and trust online and offline.

Remember... it's emotional

B2B brands aren't just expected to demonstrate purpose, they're also expected to dig even deeper into their touchy-feely sides. IBM, in an overview of general marketing trends, referred to this move as the shift from the *attention economy* to the *emotion economy*.[30]

This needn't be the big leap it appears to be. Emotion, at some level, has always sat at the heart of great marketing and advertising. Perhaps what IBM is talking about is making this much more explicit,

FIGURE 1.2 Shifting the focus of content

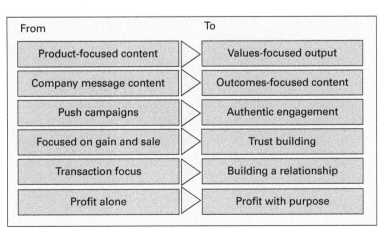

From	To
Product-focused content	Values-focused output
Company message content	Outcomes-focused content
Push campaigns	Authentic engagement
Focused on gain and sale	Trust building
Transaction focus	Building a relationship
Profit alone	Profit with purpose

as articulated emotion rather than a 'sense' or a 'feeling' of what a brand believes in or represents. As data from Google's own marketing team reveals, on average, B2B customers are significantly more emotionally connected to their vendors and service providers than consumers.[31] Of the hundreds of B2C brands studied, most had emotional connections with between 1 and 40 per cent of consumers. Meanwhile, of the nine B2B brands studied, seven surpassed the 50 per cent mark.

Heidi Taylor, in her book *B2B Marketing Strategy*, discusses the changing shape of customer engagement:

> I now look at the customer buying journey in B2B as an engagement continuum, where there are multiple potential touchpoints for both traditional and new marketing activity. Because if our customers no longer want to be sold to, we have to completely change our perspective and think not only about where along the buying journey we need to have a presence, but how we can engage with our customers before their buying journey even begins.[32]

Cross-team collaboration

If it's not already abundantly clear, the need for great brand storytelling has never been more important. The context of our storytelling is a world where we, and our potential clients and customers, are deluged with information and messaging.

Success will henceforth be all about understanding the techniques that can be leveraged to get true attention and build meaningful relationships based on a shared vision and purpose.

Success will also be about greater cross-functional collaboration. If nothing else, effective brand storytelling and brand journalism is a collaborative effort, especially now sales engagement is no longer a linear process. Because buyers will often move from digital content back to sales teams before moving closer to purchase, it's important the various teams involved recognize their own responsibilities and the way they need to collaborate with other teams:

Marketing: the marketing team guide and support commissioners and editors to create content that will align with current campaigns and business/product priorities, ensuring activity is laddering up to key marketing goals.

Communications: communications teams articulate brand messaging and re-work that into engaging messages that will appeal to target audiences and personas; the communications team will also develop tone-of-voice guidance that will underpin how stories are created and what stories you choose to tell as a brand.

Sales: communication with sales teams enables content marketers to understand the concerns of customers – what do they need to know and understand, or what are their pain points? Ideally sales would be a close partner of any editorial team developing brand journalism. Brand stories can be used as door openers and relationship starters for the sales teams themselves, as well as the basis of future collateral or lead generation collateral.

As audiences and buyers wrestle with the complex nature of our communications and marketing environment there has never been a better time to cut through with your own stories. Not only that, we are now enabled with a full range of tools to give us the ability to scope, deliver and measure every aspect of the brand stories we create and deliver. Next is to understand the facets of the newsroom you can appropriate and learn from to build a successful brand journalism strategy and production operation.

Notes

1 IBM (2017) 10 Key Marketing Trends for 2017, IBM Marketing Cloud, 3rd February. Available from: http://comsense.consulting/wp-content/uploads/2017/03/10_Key_Marketing_Trends_for_2017_and_Ideas_for_Exceeding_Customer_Expectations.pdf. (archived at https://perma.cc/3NAJ-HVZ7)

2 Dzamic, L and Kirby, J (2018) *The Definitive Guide to Strategic Content Marketing: Perspectives, issues, challenges and solutions*, Kogan Page Publishers, p 50

3 SEO Tribunal (2019) 58 amazing blogging statistics for 2019, *SEO Tribunal*, 7 February. Available from: https://seotribunal.com/blog/blogging-statistics/ (archived at https://perma.cc/B6S6-VH7L)

4 BBC (2019) Facebook tackles Russians making fake news stories, BBC News, 17 January. Available from: https://www.bbc.co.uk/news/technology-46904935 (archived at https://perma.cc/F2QR-QAZZ)

5 Barthel, M *et al* (2016) Trust, Facts and Democracy, Pew Research Centre, 7 July. Available from: https://www.journalism.org/2016/07/07/trust-and-accuracy/ (archived at https://perma.cc/X9HK-TLTU)

6 Iannopollo, E (2019) Happy data privacy day: five lessons learned on regulatory enforcement, *Forrester*, 28 January. Available from: https://go.forrester.com/blogs/happy-data-privacy-day-five-lessons-learned-on-regulatory-enforcement/ (archived at https://perma.cc/UU3C-M3XB)

7 Iannopollo, E (2018) Embrace privacy as your corporate social responsibility, *Forrester*, 19 October. Available from: https://go.forrester.com/blogs/embrace-privacy-as-your-corporate-social-responsibility-csr/ (archived at https://perma.cc/DHJ5-FT6D)

8 Iannopollo, E (2019) Happy data privacy day: five lessons learned on regulatory enforcement, *Forrester*, 28 January. Available from: https://go.forrester.com/blogs/happy-data-privacy-day-five-lessons-learned-on-regulatory-enforcement/ (archived at https://perma.cc/UU3C-M3XB)

9 Demand Gen Report (2016) Content Preferences Survey: B2B buyers value content that offers data and analysis, *Demand Gen Report*, Hasbrouck Heights, NJ. Available from: https://www.demandgenreport.com/resources/research/2016-content-preferences-survey-b2b-buyers-value-content-that-offers-data-and-analysis (archived at https://perma.cc/S9YX-JLTP)

10 Wizdo, L (2017) The ways and means of B2B buyer journey maps: we're going deep at Forrester's B2B forum, *Forrester*, 21 August. Available from: https://go.forrester.com/blogs/the-ways-and-means-of-b2b-buyer-journey-maps-were-going-deep-at-forresters-b2b-forum/ (archived at https://perma.cc/NZR2-QTTE)

11 Long, J, Roark, C and Theofilou, B (2018) The bottom line on trust, *Accenture*, 30 October. Available from: https://www.accenture.com/us-en/insights/strategy/trust-in-business (archived at https://perma.cc/D7WC-JFU4)

12 Deloitte (2019) The Deloitte Global Millennial Survey 2019, Deloitte, 20 May. Available from: https://www2.deloitte.com/global/en/pages/about-deloitte/articles/millennialsurvey.html (archived at https://perma.cc/YGL4-EJJF)

13 Demand Gen Report (2016) Content Preferences Survey: B2B buyers value content that offers data and analysis, *Demand Gen Report*, Hasbrouck Heights, NJ. Available from: https://www.demandgenreport.com/resources/

research/2016-content-preferences-survey-b2b-buyers-value-content-that-offers-data-and-analysis (archived at https://perma.cc/S9YX-JLTP)

14 Camuso, M and Ramos, L (2017) 'Crap' content continues to describe B2B marketing: don't let it describe yours, *Forrester*, 7 December. Available from: https://go.forrester.com/blogs/crap-content-continues-to-describe-b2b-marketing-dont-let-it-describe-yours/ (archived at https://perma.cc/WHX7-MK7P)

15 Smith, M (2019) Britons least likely of 22 nations to trust information on social media, *YouGov*. Available from: https://yougov.co.uk/topics/technology/articles-reports/2019/05/07/britons-least-likely-22-nations-trust-information- (archived at https://perma.cc/W9R7-JXUC)

16 Edelman (2019) 2019 Edelman Trust Barometer: Global Report, Edelman, 20 January, p 19. Available from: https://www.edelman.com/sites/g/files/aatuss191/files/2019-02/2019_Edelman_Trust_Barometer_Global_Report.pdf (archived at https://perma.cc/68U8-P5YD)

17 Spanier, G (2019) The good, the bad and the troubling: trust in advertising hits record low, *Campaign*, 30 January. Available from: https://www.campaignlive.co.uk/article/good-bad-troubling-trust-advertising-hits-record-low/1524250 (archived at https://perma.cc/9K8E-D347)

18 Oakes, O (2017) Lord Puttnam warns ad industry: trust is the most urgent task ahead, *Campaign*, 9 March. Available from: https://www.campaignlive.co.uk/article/lord-puttnam-warns-ad-industry-trust-urgent-task-ahead/1426792 (archived at https://perma.cc/HXE8-Y83C)

19 Edelman (2019) 2019 Edelman Trust Barometer: Global Report, *Edelman*, 20 January, p 34. Available from: https://www.edelman.com/sites/g/files/aatuss191/files/2019-02/2019_Edelman_Trust_Barometer_Global_Report.pdf (archived at https://perma.cc/68U8-P5YD)

20 Edelman (2017) Earned Brand Report, *Edelman*, 18 June. Available from: https://www.edelman.com/research/earned-brand-2017 (archived at https://perma.cc/CJ67-HNJE)

21 O'Brien, K (2017) How Lenovo is taking its brand beyond tech innovation, *The Drum*, 11 January. Available from: https://www.thedrum.com/news/2017/01/11/how-lenovo-taking-its-brand-beyond-tech-innovation (archived at https://perma.cc/W76H-RZY3)

22 Ritson, M (2016) If you think the sales funnel is dead, you've mistaken tactics for strategy, *Marketing Week*, 6 April. Available from: https://www.marketingweek.com/2016/04/06/mark-ritson-if-you-think-the-sales-funnel-is-dead-youve-mistaken-tactics-for-strategy/?nocache=true&login_errors%5B0%5D=invalidcombo&_lsnonce=f0c28e9876&rememberme=1&adfesuccess=1 (archived at https://perma.cc/RDS7-TQD9)

23 Catlin, T *et al* (2016) How B2B digital leaders drive five times more revenue growth than their peers, *McKinsey*, October 2016. Available from: https://www.mckinsey.com/business-functions/marketing-and-sales/our-insights/how-b2b-digital-leaders-drive-five-times-more-revenue-growth-than-their-peers (archived at https://perma.cc/ML9A-N3RA)

24 Godin, S (2018) *This is Marketing: You can't be seen until you learn to see*, *Portfolio*, p 53

25 Court, D *et al* (2009) The consumer decision journey, *McKinsey*, June 2009. Available from: https://www.mckinsey.com/business-functions/marketing-and-sales/our-insights/the-consumer-decision-journey (archived at https://perma.cc/G4VL-4G7Z)

26 Fromm, J (2019) Purpose series: a purpose-driven brand is a successful brand, *Forbes*, 16 January. Available from: https://www.forbes.com/sites/jefffromm/2019/01/16/purpose-series-a-purpose-driven-brand-is-a-successful-brand/#714fc7e6437d (archived at https://perma.cc/G89T-3QZ2)

27 Quartz Insights & WE (2019) Leading with purpose in an age defined by it, *Quartz Insights & WE*, May. Available from: https://we-worldwide-arhxo0vh6d1oh9i0c.stackpathdns.com/media/445720/we_purposeleader-190509-final.pdf (archived at https://perma.cc/ESP7-9L85)

28 Unilever (2019) Selling with Purpose, *Unilever*, 2019. Available from https://sellingwithpurpose.unilever.com/?p=252 (archived at https://perma.cc/K2HF-7UGY)

29 Fink, L (2019) Purpose & Profit, *Blackrock*. Available from: https://www.blackrock.com/corporate/investor-relations/larry-fink-ceo-letter (archived at https://perma.cc/7DYW-C4SC)

30 IBM (2018) 2019 Marketing Trends, IBM, December 2018. Available from: https://www.ibm.com/downloads/cas/RKXVLYBO (archived at https://perma.cc/7UV8-WCYU)

31 Nathan, S and Schmidt, K (2013) From promotion to emotion: connecting B2B customers to brands, *Think with Google*, October. Available from: https://www.thinkwithgoogle.com/marketing-resources/promotion-emotion-b2b/ (archived at https://perma.cc/7KTU-KBN3)

32 Taylor, H (2017) B2B *Marketing Strategy: Differentiate, develop and deliver lasting customer engagement*, Kogan Page Publishers, p 12

02

A newsroom approach: defining brand journalism for the B2B marketer

Brand journalism: a definition

There is a wide and varied selection of definitions of 'brand journalism' and the phrase divides marketers and communicators based on where they are from, whether they have been a journalist and what their exposure is to the world of content marketing. The nature of brand journalism is such that it is most obviously not about independence from power. It is, by its very nature, supported by and paid for by brands themselves. Brand journalists are *not* writing stealth content that buries a brand message and purports to be news. Instead, they are creating truly interesting stories for brands, corporates and organizations; stories that communicate a broad brand message, or value(s), but do not explicitly try to sell.

Whilst content and digital marketing has moved on markedly since he wrote about it in 2013, Andy Bull encapsulates the key attributes of what brand journalism still is today in his book, aptly titled *Brand Journalism*:

> Brand journalism is a hybrid form of traditional journalism, marketing and public relations. Brand journalism is a response to the fact that any organization can now use journalistic techniques to tell its story direct to the public.

Brand journalism's hybrid nature also sees it incorporate core elements from strategic public relations (PR) and marketing communications: visionary planning, research, incisive messages, a defined purpose, and a requirement to quantify what has been achieved through it. The result is an integrated brand journalism-driven communications strategy.[1]

For the purposes of this book, my definition is narrower, and reflects primarily sourcing and creation of top-of-funnel awareness content that does not explicitly focus or labour a brand name in any way. For me, brand journalism is, therefore:

> The creation of multi-format content, the themes of which are driven by the broad cultural, societal and business landscape, brand values and corporate purpose. Stories created are information-rich, relevant or of real value to the target audience and are created using the sensibilities, skills, tools and processes of journalism. This content is primarily uploaded on a brand's own publishing and amplification channels.

Melanie Deziel is a former journalist who founded StoryFuel, an agency supporting organizations to tell better stories. She tells me:

> I see brand journalism as a subset of all of a brand's content efforts, that lives up to the same standards of quality that we usually see in a newsroom. These standards vary widely, of course, but broadly speaking, brand journalism has a few common characteristics for me: it's content that uses reliable sources to add credibility, truly takes a unique angle or has some new perspective on a topic, and leverages some element of tension or stakes to focus on what the audience actually cares about.

Not everyone is comfortable with the idea of 'brand journalism'; amongst them is Jim Cox, a former journalist and now VP of Communications and Content at global supply chain company, Agility, who told me:

> I spent 27 years in newsrooms before leaping into corporate communications and marketing. I'm still not comfortable with the term 'brand journalism', but I don't have a better label to offer. Journalism

as I think of the term involves reporting – collecting, assembling and presenting the facts with some degree of objectivity – on matters of public interest. There's nothing preventing businesses and brands from doing the same, whether they do so on matters of broad public interest, such as climate change, or more narrowly in areas of interest to their customers and other stakeholder groups. But businesses and brands exist to sell goods and services and to maximize shareholder value, and it would be naive to think that any journalism they do isn't coloured by those underpinnings of their existence and by the marketplace imperatives that guide them.

Frictionless sharing

A feature of brand journalism is the very real likelihood that the majority of its readers will never actually be buyers. It might be they are simply part of the network that will engage with, or share, the stories, blogs or articles. That's not to underestimate them though. These people might well be the important first link in the dissemination chain – the people that start the process of sharing to a similar but broader network, and in doing so help content to be shared more widely.

The 'nodes' on this sharing network might be large (a major influencer, or a major organization), they might be small (a micro influencer perhaps), or they might be simple and linear (a click or share from an individual). But in an ideal world brands will create stories and narratives that have low friction and maximum engagement. They will *arrest the scroll* (see 'Approaches to story creation' later in this chapter), by gaining the attention of a meaningful audience and content will be shared in a frictionless fashion.

How to create brand journalism

1. Think like a journalist

While it may sound obvious to say the key requirement of writing/ commissioning brand journalism is to think like a journalist, it's not always something that comes easily to all people. This mindset requires looking for stories within your organization – stories that you can re-tell that will excite or engage your audience.

What you can do is train yourself to start asking questions that a journalist would. Even the most junior beat reporter learns to ask the *what, why, when, how?* of a story. As a communicator or marketer in your organization you can start doing the same.

As Larry Light wrote in his 2014 article on brand journalism:[2]

> Underlying brand journalism is the idea that a brand is not merely a simple word; it is a complex, multi-dimensional idea that includes differentiating features, functional and emotional benefits as well as a distinctive brand character. In this digital, mobile marketing world, no single communication can possibly relate a standardized brand message to every customer that is relevant at the right time for the right reasons. The concept is to think like a journalist.

Former *Forbes* journalist Dan Lyons famously wrote a warts-and-all book of his time as an inbound marketer and brand journalist at software company Hubspot – an organization that encourages its customers to use content marketing approaches to drive audience engagement. Whilst in the role, Lyons wrote a short treatise on the power of corporate storytelling entitled 'The CMO's Guide to Brand Storytelling'. As he so succinctly puts it: 'The media is overwhelmed and simply can't keep up. The best way to be part of the story is simply to become a journalist yourself.'[3]

If thinking like a journalist doesn't come easily, you might also want to trying building a network of other interested or engaged storytellers or evangelists in your organization. These can become key people you can turn to for more stories and insight.

Thinking like a journalist inevitably means you'll start to behave like one – including doing what all good journalists do to succeed: look out for stories in the everyday, cultivate contacts, and regularly ask around for updates on previous stories. Once you become known as the go-to person, you will invariably be approached by colleagues interested in writing for the company. While it's important not to dampen this enthusiasm, at this point it might be worth looking on your company's social media channels to see who has the knack of delivering insight and interest or thought leadership. The key message is to use these internal team members to become your first evangelists, to be your first writers or publishers and to promote the content cause.

2. Appropriate newsroom values

No-one is claiming that the type of brand journalism we are discussing here is akin to the exclusive news journalism and foreign reporting of reporters and editors at the BBC, Channel 4 News, the *Washington Post* or *The Times*. That said, what we do want is to take the best aspects and approaches of the newsroom and use those tenets and characteristics to tell great brand stories.

Any newsroom, whether for television news, newspaper or digital content, has a culture and sense of itself that will vary depending on the title, the programme and the people within it. But most newsrooms share certain values that influence the behaviours within that space.

The best journalists are, by their very nature, curious and interested people. They are interested in the world around them and the people that make the world tick. Journalists generally pride themselves on telling the news honestly as they see it, and can supplement that with context, insight and evidence for the story they are telling.

3. Don't sell, just tell

The ultimate outcome we are striving for from our brand journalism is to achieve authority and influence, deliver on specific brand messages and, in the longer term, grow sales or improve relationships with key stakeholders. In this sense, content – be it articles, blogs, videos, social media posts – needs to be uploaded and shared to owned channels.

True brand journalism is about creating and delivering stories of value to your audience, with a view to what their issues and challenges are. Your aim should be turning the focus on them, and away from your company or brand. This is how brand journalism critically differs from PR. It's about influence at the very top of, or before the start of, the sales journey – with content to be consumed at the attention and recognition stages.

FIGURE 2.1 Shifting attention to trust and advocacy

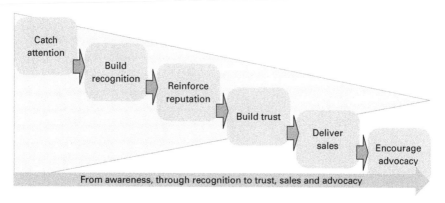

Some brands find it challenging to move away from constantly selling and pitching their own news and offerings. Mark Jones is Head of Digital Content at the World Economic Forum, and has helped to pioneer volume publishing at this international organization. He spoke to me about the Forum's success with content development and specifically about the lack of 'pure' promotion in story content.

> The brand does get 'mentioned'. Every story produced by the World Economic Forum goes out on a page with a World Economic Forum logo. It's on a website where the logo is on it. If it's in video format, it's got the World Economic Forum's logo on it. What it doesn't generally have is a great big 'sell' within it. It is getting across an idea of the Forum, showing that it is actively involved in a particular area. It's giving readers a view that there are constructed answers to some of the world's biggest problems. It's a subtle message, but one that's there.
>
> My point is simply that if you try to push a message too hard, it'll be counterproductive, especially in a world where you depend on people to share your content. They'll share it if it's interesting. They'll share it if they found it changed their point of view. They'll share it if it serves a wider purpose or if they're trying to make the world a better place themselves, but if they feel that they're being used, it's very, very hard to get people to share.

4. Be accurate and fact-based

Whatever we say on behalf of our brand has to be true, because trust – whether it's in an individual or a brand – takes a career to build up, but only a second to lose. Because we know from experience just how easily the media can get it wrong, this means sourcing facts from original sources, not just media reports. It also means being able to, where possible, back up assertions. Our brand journalist mindset should be that we *expect* to be challenged, and if we are, we should be able to defend our reporting.

Part of being objective is being able to separate personal opinions/feelings and being able to look at something from a different point of view. It should be noted, however, that this is not the same as *impartiality*. Brand journalism is – by its very nature – partial. But what it still requires is being able to look at a subject through different lenses, with the author putting themselves in other people's shoes.

Amy Hatch, a former journalist, launched the *Future of Customer Engagement and Commerce* site for SAP Customer Experience. Amy, spoke to me about the impact of her journalistic training on her approach to developing content for FCEC:

> When I was 22, I got my first local journalist job. We had our printing press on site, it was local, I wrote everything from obituaries to murder stories to state politics. I covered everything by myself for the entire community, and I think that that really informs how I approach my readership now.

> I don't think these experiences have ever left me. I think of what we do on our website as journalism. I think of it as trade journalism, and it's not a throwaway thing. It's very much around the idea of trust: putting meaningful facts into context; telling the truth; being factual and fact-checking everything we say. Today we don't say anything that is not data-driven, or if it's not data-driven, we make it very clear that this is our perspective or our writer's perspective.

We only have eight seconds to engage a reader, so we put the most important information at the top of the story. We use the inverted pyramid method of storytelling; it's the very straightforward stuff that they teach you in journalist school, that I don't think all marketers have in their back pocket.

The structure behind our beautiful content is highly disciplined, it has a moral compass, and it's really about truth and facts in context that resonate with people.

Every piece of content we have comes from the same foundations. There's nothing in it that betrays that ethos, and that takes a lot of work.

5. Develop a journalistic process

Every newsroom is built on efficiency. Without clear structure, planning and a ruthless attachment to process, it would be impossible to create ongoing daily content of consistent quality. This applies to whether the output produced is tabloid in nature, in-depth or otherwise; this structure enables any publication to create a range of output, and be able to respond to breaking news as it happens. Brand journalism, however, is not about breaking news. It is about uncovering feature stories and brand stories that continuously reflect the nature of the organization.

Even if you cannot afford to create a dedicated newsroom for your content marketing, it is still possible to pull together a certain amount of resource to create content on a consistent, daily or weekly basis. You just have to have a plan and then stick to it.

NEWSROOM TIP
Work to a deadline

There's nothing like a hard deadline to encourage efficiency and effective resource utilization. If you can set and hit deadlines when you're planning your organization's content – even if they are for your own internal purposes – you will build a more efficient system and process within your organization.

Set the system up properly and the output will follow. Whether large or small, make sure you're organized, with rigorous approaches to planning, process and people. There's nothing like a system to improve efficiency, manage your resources better and deliver a flow of quality content.

6. Don't just be aware, be interested

This might sound obvious, but if you want to talk to your various audiences about the issues that are vexing them in their own industries, it's essential you know what you are talking about. You (and your team) need to understand the issues and stories that are impacting the world as a whole. Try to become acquainted with the specialist technical areas that you work in. It may well be you are developing wider 'insight' stories (thought leadership on management or leadership techniques), but this doesn't change the fact that the context of what you are writing is the world around us.

If you are looking for *Journalism 101* tips on how to get started, keep the following actions in mind:

- **Subscribe and ingest:** read widely and in depth. Make sure you have trustworthy sources for your general news and information; be well versed in the politics, economics and context of today's complex business world.

- **Talk and engage with your people:** your organization's experts are an incredibly accessible group of people that can feed your knowledge and understanding of a sector. Talk to them when you can, read their commentaries, reports, articles and social media posts.

- **Build specialist expertise:** even if you are in a communications or marketing position, start to develop your own expertise and interest in key areas. If you have a team of in-house writers or freelance journalists, become as expert as them. Subscribe to specialist B2B papers and newsletters to update and freshen your knowledge.

- **Attend industry events:** there is nothing like specialist B2B events to really revive your knowledge and insight in a particular industry.

There are thousands of these to attend each year, but the leading industry events are generally well known and attract leading thinkers on multiple subject areas. Attending them can be well worth the investment.

7. Be responsive

Much of what we see on our nightly news bulletins or on our online news pages is actually fairly well planned – for instance, a visit by a president, a celebration around a milestone event, a diary story or the findings of a piece of research.

In addition to these scheduled events, newsrooms also respond to breaking news on the day. In a newsroom, a story will change with each new piece of evidence or insight that is gathered; the focus will change as interviewees reveal new information. Speed, therefore, is of the essence, as is an ability to gather and assimilate the facts.

As brand journalists you should look to appropriate this responsiveness and speed. That's not to say that you need to respond to every event, or create 'breaking news' content – but it does mean that you should understand and analyse what is happening in the broader world environment as well as in the particular industries in which you are working. Focus on the changes and challenges being felt inside the companies you are working with. For instance, if world trade is slowing and it will impact container trade, freight, supply chains – what kind of stories can you tell within that environment to reflect those challenges?

CASE STUDY
Newsjacking to build engagement

Newsjacking is a term used to describe taking advantage of current events to publicize your brand. When done well, events can be used to develop new or fresh angles or stories. For instance, if you know your audience is talking about the World Economic Forum in Davos and the key discussion points being raised there, this can be a good time to engage in the debate. In fact, rather than shying away from news events you should be actively seeking these opportunities.

The simplest example of 'newsjacking' is the use of anniversaries, birthdays and memorial dates to revisit an event from the past in order to review or analyse an activity, industry or sector. Take a recent story from the World Economic Forum entitled 'What is going on in Chernobyl today?' The article performed extremely well on the World Economic Forum's *Agenda* website, primarily because it tapped into audience engagement that had been stirred up by a recent TV mini-series on the incident. So the popularity of the post wasn't simply driven by the reference to the incident, but to a popular culture drama that emerged from it.

HOW DO YOU NEWSJACK SUCCESSFULLY?

- **Be clever:** don't be lazy about taking an event and building on it – especially if the event is a negative or devastating one. Be insightful and sophisticated about how to use a news event, memory, anniversary or trend to develop strong material for your brand.

- **Be sensitive and mature:** aim to be sensitive to how you are referencing the source material, and ensure the tone of voice correlates to the tone required for coverage of that particular topic. Consider whether your story will cause offence.

- **Be quick:** turn out your content quickly to ensure you make the most of any conversation that's out there and trending.

- **Be SEO clever:** use your Google search and tools such as AnswerThePublic[4] – the data visualization tool that fetches and maps keyword suggestions and predictions from a world of Google searches. Once identified, dig deep on these keywords, or other lines you can follow.

8. Consistency, commitment and agility

In a typical newsroom, the production system never breaks down, or has off days. Those that work in news soon get used to this 'always on' approach, and it's one brand journalists should try to replicate too.

This isn't about a 'set and forget' approach to content delivery and engaging with audiences. It's about listening to the conversation and responding. Some might call it being agile, but whatever you choose to call it, you need to live and breathe the stories you are telling for brands to audiences.

Consistency and commitment are key when producing branded content; this is a long game that you need to commit time and resources to for the long term, as part of your marketing mix. It's not an approach that will bear fruit overnight, but will gradually build organic audiences over time.

Companies delivering great brand journalism demonstrate a structured commitment to create, publish and amplify great content to draw potential customers or clients closer to their brand. Owned media platforms are the primary home for brand journalism content – but stories can be leveraged across paid, earned and social sites.

9. Quality over quantity

Organizations that espouse the benefits of brand journalism often operate and commit to publishing at scale, with tactics informed by data and insight.

But how many articles or pieces of content should you publish to gain and maintain an audience? In a perfect world we would all have the budget to produce high quantities of content, but in reality, budgets and resources are often tight. On average, only three articles were uploaded each week to IQ's Intel site before it was shuttered – the focus was on quality over quantity. SAP's *Future of Customer Engagement and Commerce* site publishes an average five articles each week. The World Economic Forum, meanwhile, publishes dozens each day.

It's worth remembering most largescale brand publishers focus on creating high-quality articles – because quality pieces can be updated or can be re-surfaced as evergreen content (which actually boosts your publishing cadence if the high cost of original content is a challenge for your brand). Even engaged readers will consume five to seven pieces of content before they move into the 'support or inform' stage of the buying process, ie before they become an opportunity.[5]

That means you need to keep serving up regular, interesting, new, but also quality brand journalism to keep audiences engaged. I spoke to content marketing expert and author Robert Rose about his view on where B2B brands can improve their approach to content development and commitment to publication:

> What most brands miss is they don't build a platform. They don't build a publication. They don't build a 'centre of gravity' around their content. What they do is just build asset after asset after asset that lives in a disaggregated format on their website.
>
> What people don't subscribe to are individual pieces of content. They subscribe to something that they're going to keep getting. This is what creating and building an audience is all about, and it's what most brands, quite frankly, don't do.
>
> Most brands look at content as an asset that drives a transaction, which for them might be a registration or an entry in my marketing database. They call that an audience. But that's not an audience, that's just somebody who transacted for a piece of content!

10. Have a consistent tone, look and feel

Just as every news programme is different, complete with a different slant, focus or set of production values, so your own corporate content must reflect your own brand or company. This means the tone and image of what you produce – on every channel – must reflect your values, and must appeal to your target audience. Once you establish what this is (a good tip is to come up with a short paragraph explaining what you are trying to do with your content), you must then ensure it's consistent. Consistency means from a tone of voice, language and design point of view. Not only will this give cohesion to your content, it will ensure it stands out in the huge flow of information we are delivered each day.

Approaches to story creation

Good brand journalism shares some key storytelling techniques that are worth considering before you commission or create your first article, video or podcast.

Step 1: Have the audience in mind

Your stories should reflect the particular audience you are speaking to. They should reflect the things the audience is talking about, and the concerns they have, or the challenges they face. Having an audience in mind is less about thinking, 'What story do we want to tell?' or 'What message do we want to send?'; it focuses on the pivotal questions of, 'What parts of the story will people engage with?' and 'How do we get that message across?'

Answering these questions requires understanding that different audiences want, like and react to things in different ways. There is never one size fits all.

PERSONA DEVELOPMENT

Traditionally, one way of categorizing different audiences, and making sure you are aligned to their values, is to create personas for your audiences. In theory, the simple act of creating a character gives more detail about who they are, where they come from, what age they are and what roles they are in.

PERSONA DEVELOPMENT – A STARTING POINT

Role: key information about role, company, size, type of company, location etc.

Demographic information: age, gender, income, marital status, location, work location, family size, education status.

Status and challenges: range of goals and challenges at work or in role; our/vendor solution to these problems.

However, it's worth remembering that these sorts of facts do not always give a clear view of what motivates a person. Personas can be fleshed out more fully using:

- **Quantitative research:** ideally you will use research from your sales teams, from your own organization and from your usage and archive data to get a sense of who you are talking to, what their habits are, where they interact (online and offline) and what 'makes them tick'.

- **Qualitative research:** interviews with clients and customers give a more nuanced understanding of who you are talking to and what their needs and values are. You can also glean a stronger sense of what type of information and content they will be interested in. Renew and update your research when you can.

- **First-person understanding:** visit sample target audience profiles on LinkedIn and Twitter to see what your audience shares, when and to whom. Get a sense of what they value by what stories they endorse or comment on. Quickly you can refine your understanding of their world view.

If you put your audience first, you will always have them at the heart of your storytelling, and will be able to maintain the quality of your content as you need to build an ongoing audience. You must aim to develop what social media marketing consultant and author Mark Schaefer[6] calls an *Alpha Audience* – this is 'an elite and engaged tribe at the top of the social sharing food chain, the bedrock of your business'.

According to Schaefer, this Alpha Audience will be active and engaged with your content, even if it's just sharing it on social media, and it builds the thing we all aspire to creating – trust. 'Trust,' says Schaefer, 'is the launch code for the Alpha Audience rocket. Trust cements you to the only people who truly matter in your digital world.'[7]

GROWING YOUR AUDIENCE

- **Inform:** be a source of information and insight your audiences can rely on.
- **Analyse:** keep on top of what they like, what's working, what's not.
- **Experiment:** try new approaches to your content; if they don't work, re-group and try again.

- **Respond:** reply and respond to comments on your content where possible; moderate where you can. When, or if, your community becomes big enough, you can often look to them to respond on your behalf.
- **Collaborate:** ask your audience for guidance and support.
- **Paid:** support key pieces of quality content with targeted paid promotion to highlight the best of what you have to new followers or audience members.

Step 2: Arrest the scroll

The stories you focus on should be developed to attract your audience and *arrest the scroll* when they are flicking through the deluge of information that is served to them on their social media and web channels. At its most basic, arresting the scroll means grabbing your audience's attention. But it's important your brand journalism contains certain characteristics to get them to notice what you have to say, whatever format it's in. These are:

Offer value: the value of your content is that which delivers value. Robert Rose maintains you can engage audiences (and bring them into an early trust relationship) with your brand at the search phase, before they even have a perceived need. If you tell them interesting and useful information, they'll be inclined to have a trust-based relationship with you right from the start.

Be credible: anything you create should deliver information or insight. Therefore it must be based on research and knowledge, no matter how short or long. One well-researched piece that is credible, shareable and original will travel further through your target networks.

Be interesting: use strong headlines, clear images and punchy vocabulary to draw in your audience via social media and promotion, then present intriguing articles that are easy to scan, optimistic and simple to digest. I will cover story structure later in the book, but top stories on the World Economic Forum's *Agenda* site include list-structure stories that outline, in an easy-to-digest way, the world's leading countries on a range of different topics. They are insightful, but straightforward to digest.

Add drama: don't be afraid of adding a bit of drama. When dealing with drier, more detail-focused content, such as some more complex B2B topics, it's more important than ever to make sure you bring these subjects to life. Add context where you can, add insight or colour to the stories you are telling. Build tension and a hero/challenge/resolution story arc if possible. If not, find other techniques or mechanisms to engage.

Step 3: Put humans at the centre

Making your storytelling more *human* will always improve your communication with the audience – because it helps the message stick and aids cut-through.

Ideally you will identify a way to tell your story through a human example or case study. Ask, for example, if there is one person that exemplifies the narrative or demonstrates the point you are trying to make and the impact it is having on a real audience or group of people. Find out more about story structure and human examples later in the book.

NEWSROOM TIP
Be personal

For the World Economic Forum's *Agenda* site, successful headlines are short, sharp, carefully written and often focused on personal experience, or on the direct human impact of activity. For instance, it runs pieces entitled 'How you talk to your child changes their brain',[8] or on one person's view or approach: 'What Croatia's president taught the world about leadership at the World Cup'.[9]

Even if you do not feel confident in yourself as a 'brand journalist', getting to grips with the techniques of the newsroom can underpin your entire approach to top-of-funnel content marketing and content creation. Before you create any content, you should first confirm and agree your strategy, map your resources and establish the best formats and platforms for your target audience.

Notes

1 Bull, A (2013) *Brand Journalism*, Routledge, p 1
2 Light, L (2014) Brand Journalism: How to engage successfully with consumers in an age of inclusive individuality, *Journal of Brand Strategy*, **3** (2), pp 121–28
3 Lyons, D (2013) The CMO's guide to brand journalism, *HubSpot*. Available from: https://www.hubspot.com/cmos-guide-to-brand-journalism (archived at https://perma.cc/3BC3-BSZ7)
4 Answer The Public (nd) Available from: https://answerthepublic.com/ (archived at https://perma.cc/Z7S6-VWLV)
5 Interview with Amy Hatch for this book, referring to SAP website: *Future of Customer Engagement and Commerce*
6 Schaefer, M W (2015) *The Content Code: Six essential strategies to ignite your content, your marketing, and your business*, Mark W Schaefer, p 97
7 Schaefer, M W (2015) *The Content Code: Six essential strategies to ignite your content, your marketing, and your business*, Mark W Schaefer, p 109
8 Hardach, S (2018) How you talk to your child changes their brain, *World Economic Forum*, 28 February. Available from: https://www.weforum.org/agenda/2018/02/how-you-talk-to-your-child-changes-their-brain/ (archived at https://perma.cc/9X5U-2VN4)
9 Purtill, C (2018) What Croatia's president taught the world about leadership at the World Cup, *World Economic Forum*, 17 July. Available from: https://www.weforum.org/agenda/2018/07/croatia-s-president-taught-a-lesson-in-leadership-at-the-world-cup/ (archived at https://perma.cc/97B8-5B2X)

03

Building your storytelling strategy

Great brand journalism stories speak for themselves. They play a pivotal role at the start of the customer journey, supporting lead generation and purchase reinforcement. They also create advocacy and help brands build customers from audiences over time.

Yet by the same token, great stories cannot always be easily surfaced. As previous chapters have referenced, they need to appeal to the right customer base; they have to engage with audiences personally (be this through tone, format or values), and just as importantly, they must work at scale in supporting customers as they move through the buyer cycle.

But perhaps more important than any of these is the fact that any brand journalism journey has to make having a clear strategy its core foundation.

To anyone still unsold on the virtues of brand journalism, a documented approach will also enable you to sell your concept to senior internal stakeholders – those people who sign off the budget you will need to deliver on your aspirations.

Creating your approach

To support the customer sales journey, your brand journalism ultimately needs to support broader brand objectives, alongside any specific tactical or campaign aspirations. The best strategies will take a step-by-step approach, as shown in Figure 3.1.

FIGURE 3.1 Story publication: an ongoing process

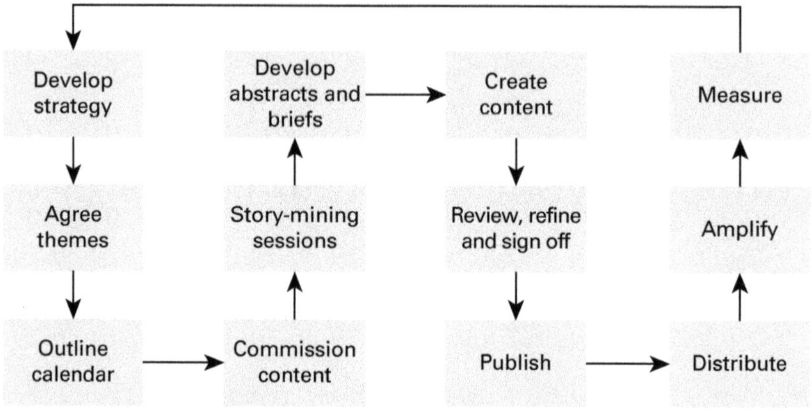

Develop strategy	Develop abstracts and briefs	Create content	Measure
Agree themes	Story-mining sessions	Review, refine and sign off	Amplify
Outline calendar	Commission content	Publish	Distribute

Define your goals and outcomes

Building a content marketing strategy supported by brand journalism is an approach that will build engagement over time. Creating meaningful relationships online through engaging storytelling will not happen overnight. Your approach will be determined by the aims and aspirations. It might well be that your brand is adjusting how it is viewed by external stakeholders and audiences; you might want to shift perception of the brand, or be launching into a new market or product offering.

Before you start, consider:

- What do we want to achieve with this content strategy?
- Where does it fit into our overarching marketing planning?
- Which other partners will need to be included in delivering the plan?
- Who are the key stakeholders and how do each of them need to be engaged?
- How will content support your wider communications planning?
- What do you want audiences to think, feel and do?
- How long is content needed for?
- How does this content fit with long- and short-term goals?
- How will you measure your success?

FIGURE 3.2 Building a content strategy

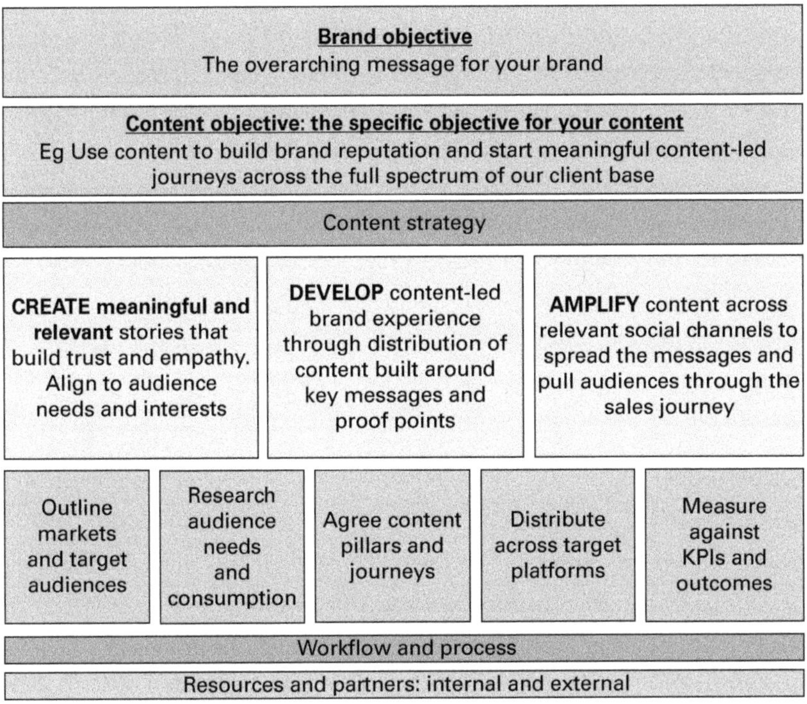

As your brand journalism develops, aims can shift, to move beyond working simply at the start of the customer journey to support engagement with sales and marketing teams, or more focused demand and lead generation activity. It's therefore vital that aims are continually revisited and continually assessed to see if they support the entire customer journey.

CASE STUDY
Centrica

UK-based energy and services multinational Centrica chose to develop a brand journalism hub called Stories to broaden its reputation away from a traditional utility. Its approach was driven by a desire to disintermediate and to control how the brand message landed to target audiences, as Laura Price, former Centrica Director of Digital Communications, explains:

> Centrica had to find a different way of reaching the audiences that we wanted to speak to, whether that's an investor audience, a political one, or even the media. For us it was a natural pathway to mediating our own communication because essentially it was getting increasingly difficult to use the media as our mouthpiece. With digital delivery, you've got complete control over the message, which is so opposite to a traditional channel where you talk to a journalist and then they put the story out that they want to write or they think's going to sell their paper.

> We were taking on something quite different in terms of an approach. It's not something that we've ever done before with Centrica; we've never told stories, we've simply reported corporate news. We wanted to put Centrica in a space with some of the new and emerging technology companies that our business is competing with right now.

Use storytelling and brand journalism content across the entire sales journey – but focus on where it will have the biggest impact.

According to research by McKinsey:

> B2B organizations need to develop a much deeper understanding of the modern Customer Decision Journey (CDJ). Where the old sales funnel assumed a linear purchasing path – customers take in information, narrow down their choices, kick the tyres, and submit the purchase order – the CDJ moves away from the 'funnel' way of doing things. It recognizes that the decision process is, in fact, anything but linear, and the post-purchase period is often as or more important than other steps along the way.

What the McKinsey research tells us is that content will need to gain the attention of, and influence, a much wider range of different stakeholders, from 'strangers' to 'post purchasers' (see table), each with different needs, requirements and issues. It indicates that once a customer has bought into your product or service – often over a long

TABLE 3.1 The evolution of brand journalism at different stages of the customer journey

Stage in customer journey	The role of brand journalism	Content recommendations
Pre-awareness and awareness	Our content needs to REACH a broad audience of our targets and their networks.	General insight articles, trends output, global themes content including videos.
	Will our audiences share those stories across their networks?	Thought leadership and opinion pieces, podcasts and livestreaming or live event broadcast to demonstrate insights.
		Personal value narratives and stories engage potential clients with our senior leadership.
		Longer articles and white papers can draw in specialist audiences.
Interest	Content needs to ENGAGE people in order to build brand recognition.	Business- and topic-focused articles, white papers, videos and ebooks support sales engagement and calls.
	Do our values and approaches match those of our audience?	Live coverage and reporting on social channels covering specific events, campaigns or target business areas.
Consideration	To become a real consideration, brands need to prove they UNDERSTAND a buyer's needs, problems to be solved and belief system.	Continued insight delivery plus case study and proof point focus amplified via social media channels.
	To build trust, brands and individuals must SHARE values, beliefs and expectations.	Ongoing email newsletters deliver a regular digest of brand journalism stories to segmented audiences.
		Ongoing social posting, targeting and sharing amplifies your messages.

(continued)

TABLE 3.1 (Continued)

Stage in customer journey	The role of brand journalism	Content recommendations
Purchase	To make a sale, brands need to CONVINCE people of their value.	Webinars, live event engagement and more detailed case studies and proof points focus on technical details and queries. Trials, face-to-face sales engagement, product demos, Q&A and specifications reassure and offer more detail.
Post-purchase	Brands need to REASSURE people they've made the right decision by exceeding expectations through actions. Where possible they must NURTURE this new relationship to build clients into advocates for the brand.	Continued email marketing with relevant, personalized material tells clients about ongoing innovation, research and change. Continued reinforcement of corporate values and beliefs encourages advocacy and brand building or case study development with clients. Podcast content, live coverage and reporting on social channels tell clients we are across new developments in influential global events and the industry.

period of time – upselling and retention are just as important. Here, timely and regular stories will be required that resonate with your buyers and customers, to reinforce their purchase decision as well as encourage them to share your content across their own networks – this time as advocates for your brand.

The content archetype approach

For those who feel that the sales funnel and customer journey model is too structured a way to approach your brand journalism and content marketing, there are other approaches. Strategic advisory firm Altimeter has segmented content strategy into five *archetypes*[1] that help define the end use or aim of content, and they can be used in place of a sales funnel or customer journey model:

Content as *Presence*: this is where content is focused on demonstrating broad awareness of your brand. Your audience is wide, and your subjects are general and broad in appeal. The World Economic Forum pursues this approach with its volume publishing model.

Content as *Currency*: this is when your organization delivers content of value, either professionally or personally. Content supports your audience by helping them make a decision in their life. It will help make the brand a trusted partner or thought leader. As an example, strategic advisor McKinsey puts thought leadership front and centre on its main website. The content is regular and of high quality, based on research and insight across all its multiple segments of expertise. Commercial data company Dun & Bradstreet similarly produces regular 'expert insights for business leaders' on its Perspectives hub,[2] focusing on sales and marketing skills, data management, procurement and compliance challenges.

Content as a *Window*: this is when companies tell the stories about their people or products to demonstrate transparency and build credibility with audiences. This approach is a great way to build trust in your brand. As more brands focus on purpose, building trust, and demonstrating the culture of their organizations, this type of content will become more instrumental in the future for delivering key messages.

Content as *Community*: this is when companies create platforms where their network (or community) can discuss and engage, as well as respond to content created. American Express content site Open Forum was a benchmark of community building through content, providing support and guidance to thousands of small business customers and hub members. The site has now been integrated into the American Express main website as Business Trends and Insights, but it continues to add value to a targeted small business audience.[3]

Content as *Support*: this is when content has an educational purpose. The style will be more 'how to' in nature and it supports and informs a very specific need. Content like this complements retention strategies as a hygiene factor on your website, delivering tactical information around the key questions current clients might have.

Map your audience

Whatever you want to achieve, it's crucial you develop clear descriptions of who you are talking to with your brand journalism and storytelling. At the back of your mind, with any piece of content, you should always ask: 'Why will my target audiences be interested in what we have to say?' or 'What do I want my audiences to think, feel and do?'

To answer these questions, as you will have read in the previous chapter, you must first establish your customers' personas and needs and map them against your own business aspirations (for instance building trust, driving reputation, reducing time to sale). This will determine which type of content you should prioritize and focus attention on to best fulfil both sets of requirements.

As we have learned, it is not simply about creating a demographic or quantitative list of the characteristics of your target audience(s). What matters most is what matters to them. If you're going to develop stories that resonate with people, you need to understand their very personal drivers, beliefs and challenges. There are a number of techniques you can use to establish this.

Mine audience outputs to create insights

Personas based on a broad set of information (such as need state, position in the sales journey, role, challenges, and demographics) are fine, but you need to dig more deeply to get a more rounded picture. For instance, what issues are your audiences interested in, or what do they feel motivated by?

You can uncover this type of insight by tracking the activity of your target audiences on social media sites, and seeing what type of content they are sharing and commenting on. Right now this is a whole emerging science around the 'psychology of social sharing', including a recent *New York Times*-commissioned study with Customer Insight Group and Latitude Research. Previous research has also revealed that the top three types of social content shared are blog articles, visuals and comments. So, research the Twitter and Instagram accounts of key targets and export them into spreadsheets where you can review keywords, common phrases and repeated commentary. You can read more about audience understanding in the next chapter.

Remember though, you are not looking to mention products, product launches or news from your company; you are looking to match the interests and needs of your audiences.

Focus on adding value

Your aim is not just to service a core audience with your stories and brand journalism; it is to deliver content that will be part of the broader customer experience and can be shared to a broader network, reinforcing a brand message for you throughout multiple arenas or networks.

The best way to ensure success with audiences is by giving them something of value. According to those surveyed by Altimeter in 2018, high-value content is that which helps the customer make a decision (both personally and professionally), and promotes the brand as a subject matter expert. This type of content worked best for those interviewed from service-oriented industries like banking, healthcare and technology.[4]

So, choose areas where people need or want to gain knowledge or insight, or where they have specific challenges/pain points in broader business terms. There is scope here for companies – even those who are ultimately trying to sell a service or product – to become a trusted source of information. Some 90 per cent of those interviewed for the Demand Gen Report's 2019 Content Preferences Survey[5] said they

FIGURE 3.3 Understanding your audiences

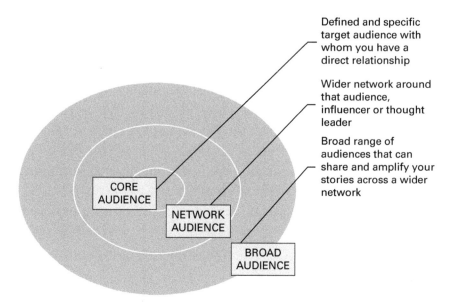

Defined and specific target audience with whom you have a direct relationship

Wider network around that audience, influencer or thought leader

Broad range of audiences that can share and amplify your stories across a wider network

would consider vendor content as trustworthy, whilst 68 per cent said they wanted content grouped around an issue, challenge or pain point.

If your aim is to build brand awareness with engaging top-of-funnel and pre-funnel brand journalism, you will have an even broader canvas of content areas from which to choose that might interest your audiences. Your ultimate goal should be to pique an interest with a story that engages or informs.

Create themed content

Segmenting your content into themes will help audiences better navigate your content, and will allow you to promote it more efficiently. Rather than taking your internal structures or divisions as a theme structure, begin with your audience needs, groups or verticals.

Here are some ways in which B2B content hubs in the technology and financial services sectors have segmented their content into themes to reflect specific verticals, audience needs or challenges. Ideally you should not create themes that simply reflect your internal corporate structure or divisions, as these do not always reflect your audiences' key drivers:

- **Aon's *The One Brief*.**[6] This site delivers its content under the catch-all heading of 'The world's most pressing business issues' and covers industry-changing macro trends in 'Capital & Economics', wellbeing and workforce trends in 'People & Organizations', and challenges to global business in 'Risk & Innovation'. Using a range of formats (graphics, imagery, original design), as well as social sharing tools on each blog article, *The One Brief* encourages sharing amongst target audiences.
- **Fujitsu's I-Global Intelligence for the CIO.**[7] Covers business issues and peer-to-peer debate on business and technology trends to appeal to CIOs themselves or their influencer networks. Content is grouped into strategy, management, innovation and thought leadership (called 'Big Thinkers').
- **SAP's *Future of Customer Engagement and Commerce*.**[8] Here, content is grouped around the themes of commerce, customer experience, service, sales, marketing and purpose. Some of those are more closely aligned to the SAP product than others, but half are focused on broad areas of insight and learning (sales, service, marketing), whilst one harnesses the interest in brand purpose, covering topics such as diversity, gender equality and broad thought leadership topics.

Agree your style and tone

Your verbal or written identity speaks volumes about who you are as a brand. Landing the right tone of voice – one that sits with the image you want to create, and doesn't jar with existing style guides – is an art form any brand journalist has to master and then stay consistent with to get the cut-through they want. It's likely a tone of voice document will already exist – developed by your communications team or the marketing team as part of the corporate communications toolkit – but based on your new stated aims for our brand journalism, it might need updating.

If you need to develop an approach from scratch, you should consider:

Drivers	Detail
Tone	Your tone of voice is 'how' you speak and can often be driven by or guided by your values. You might be human, approachable, efficient – and therefore you might want to engage with audiences in a relaxed but direct way.
	You might be, like MailChimp, committed to speaking like an 'experienced and compassionate business partner' who doesn't take himself very seriously, so injects humour into his words.[9]
	But it may well be that your brand needs to be smart and innovative. Whatever the requirement, ensure your content contains or reflects those keywords or maxims in all the content you create.
	Consider creating a list of 'yes' words – words you will use for your brand writing – and 'no' words – those that don't support your guidelines.
Language	What level of audience are you pitching your content at? Who will read it and what kind of tone will they relate to?
	Remember, you need to make your content readable and accessible and encourage 'frictionless sharing'.
	Our recommendation is to keep your language as accessible as possible. People reading online tend to read more slowly than they do reading from standard print. Keep your sentences short and your language as simple as possible, whilst aiming to get your message across clearly and precisely.
Technicality	How much technical information do you wish to include, or how much detail on any subject that you are covering?
	Steer away from technical language where possible. Obviously if you are creating technical content, you will need to reference specifics, but if you are writing on broader topics, or industry-wide content that is relevant for a broad audience, limit your technical content and explain what you need to with a glossary.
Localization and translation	Many markets need content or stories 'localized' to reflect the true issues of that region or area. Do not overlook the need for local knowledge if specific audiences have tailored needs.
	Do not believe that you can simply translate your available content into local languages; often content and stories will need recreating or developing from scratch for specific locations. One option is to use template base copy and then drop in localized quotes and insight if producing stories for multiple regions or geographies.

SAP's Customer Experience content hub, the *Future of Customer Engagement and Commerce*, had a clear 'voice' from the start, says Amy Hatch when interviewed for this book:

One of the reasons this site is so successful is because it has a personality, it has a tone. When you read it, it's got heart and soul, it feels very human, it doesn't feel sterile and it feels genuine, authentic and it's very transparent. We're not trying to be something we're not.

The site very much reflects who the team is. It can be a double-edged sword, because you have to continually find people to help run that strategy who have that mindset, but we have a really special chemistry in our team. Our internal subject matter experts have cultivated knowledge over many years. It's a long game, so you have to have a leadership that's educated and that understands what you are trying to do.

Find your rhythm

When you're looking to enhance and encourage maximum sharing with your content, finding subjects that resonate with your target audience is essential. On GE's content marketing hub *GE Reports*, the subjects it focuses on are aviation, digital, healthcare, energy, and advanced manufacturing – all under the overarching primary theme of 'Innovation'. Editor in Chief at GE, Tomas Kellner,[10] leads the team that publishes the GE Reports website and newsletter. He says stories that tend to work best are larger themes GE has a connection to, such as climate change and renewables in energy, for instance. As stories are topical and broad, he sees his competition as the *Wall Street Journal* rather than content from GE competitors.

Formats: no right or wrong

While stories themselves might chop and change, there is no right or wrong when it comes to choosing your formats, and there is no 'one size fits all' approach to how you structure your stories.

If you have already started producing content, then you will probably have a sense of what works and what does not. It could well be that your audiences prefer video to the written word or have shown a particular interest in podcasts as a channel for specialist insight.

From here you will be able to analyse in great detail whether it's short-form video or longer-form content that works better, and what style of text copy is more appealing.

If you have not started on the brand journalism journey yet, then you will need to review content as you go and test your format ranges for popularity. As well as measuring appeal and popularity of the content in terms of readership, completion time and bounce rate for individual pages, you should also look for the crucial sharing metrics. Remember, the aim is to encourage frictionless sharing of your content across your audience networks.

Broadly, visual content and video are growing in popularity because they are appealing and easy to digest (and share). Their merits will be covered in more detail in later chapters, but at this point, simply ensure you are thinking broadly about what you will produce. Do not simply focus on text alone.

A regular publishing cadence

Ideally you want to have consistent, ongoing content delivered to your site on a regular basis – what's often called 'drumbeat content' – supported by shorter, focused 'campaigns' based around key themes, target audiences, events or outcomes.

Naturally, publishing frequency will always be dictated by resources and budget, but regularity does breed readership. When thinking about your own drumbeat, you need to think about how you schedule not only your regular drumbeat content but your sporadic themed material additional to this, and specific campaigns (see Figure 3.4).

Regular drumbeat content

This is your ongoing, consistent pulse of content delivered at your own pace and rhythm. In an ideal world you would publish quality content to a content hub or your blog site as often as daily (as in a newsroom), but for many brands the reality is one new quality article each week, with only high-volume publishers delivering more.

FIGURE 3.4 Drumbeat content at the heart of regular output

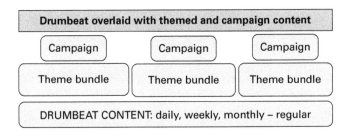

As you build up an archive of material over time, you could always consider re-purposing and re-posting material that has worked well in the past with audiences, amplifying it with updated social media content as required. Often archive material will supplement your SEO activities and continue to drive meaningful traffic volumes.

Ideally, drumbeat content comprises stories that address the key concerns or needs of your audience, but can still live in your archive for some time into the future. Articles and topical blogs will form the bedrock of most drumbeat content. These are relatively cost-effective to create and can fit into a regular rhythm of commissioning. However, drumbeat content could just as easily be in a video format, or podcast, or long-form, if you feel that is what your audience will be receptive to.

Curation in the mix

If you are considering a high-volume approach to a specific hub, you might want to consider the cost-effective approach of curating specific pieces of content from strategic partners. Source key publishing partners who you believe will be a good fit for your brand and who are already creating the sort of content you feel would work on your own hub or site. Ideally you will also create a limited volume of curated material alongside your own original content. If you are planning to curate content from other sources, make sure you consider some key factors:

- **Brand alignment:** is the content you are posting aligned in vision and values to your own brand?

- **Value-add:** is the content delivering insight to the end user? Will it chime with the aspiration and mission of your content hub?

- **Quality:** is it well written/edited and regularly delivered? Are you able to change, re-write or subedit the content or does it need to be published in its entirety?

- **Promotion:** what kind of promotion or reference does any partner expect from your publication of the content?

If your site becomes popular and successful as a standalone engagement hub for key audiences (for instance, Adobe's *CMO.com*) you might well find brands approach you with content that they would like to have posted. The World Economic Forum has built a high-volume, high-quality audience for its on-site *Agenda* platform and is in the lucky position of being able to agree publishing arrangements with global thought leaders, associations and academic institutions. This enables the Forum to have a pool of more than 600 articles each day from which it can choose a handful to publish that fulfil its quality and content criteria, supporting its volume content aspirations.

Thematic packages

FIGURE 3.5 The content theme bundle

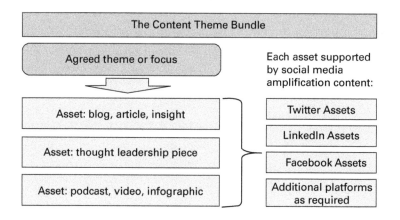

Regular drumbeat content can be supplemented with additional content packages that reflect a specific theme, challenge or area of focus. A bundle can be created around a sales push or product where the broad journalistic messaging drives readers further into the sales funnel with links to additional insight.

Content can be developed as one larger 'cornerstone' piece that harnesses a key thought or focus for your business. This can then be 'atomized' or split up into smaller, snackable pieces of content that will be supported by amplification – either paid or organic – across your target audience channels. Entrepreneur and digital marketing evangelist Gary Vaynerchuk uses this approach comprehensively for his content and for clients, calling it the 'pillar model'. He explains that he starts with a piece of pillar content – for him always a video – and then his team creates dozens of smaller pieces of content from that, contextualized according to which platform they are uploaded to.

Remember, however, to be flexible with your approach. As channels and formats change and proliferate, what is popular today might not be popular in the very near future.

As you build up your content and develop a production flow, you can begin to analyse which formats and types of content are more successful with your audiences and mould your future content plans accordingly. Build a repeat schedule, enabling you to stretch timeless content and leverage your archive.

Adrian Monck is a Managing Director at the World Economic Forum. In an interview for this book he explained how his team used original material and a robust repeat schedule to develop and grow the Forum's popular *Agenda* site with a broad and engaged global audience:

> If a story doesn't resonate today, it might next month, it might strike a chord in six months' time. We regularly see stories that perhaps didn't perform as well as expected when they were first published being brought to life because they happened to capture something that is suddenly relevant.

FIGURE 3.6 An indicative publication schedule

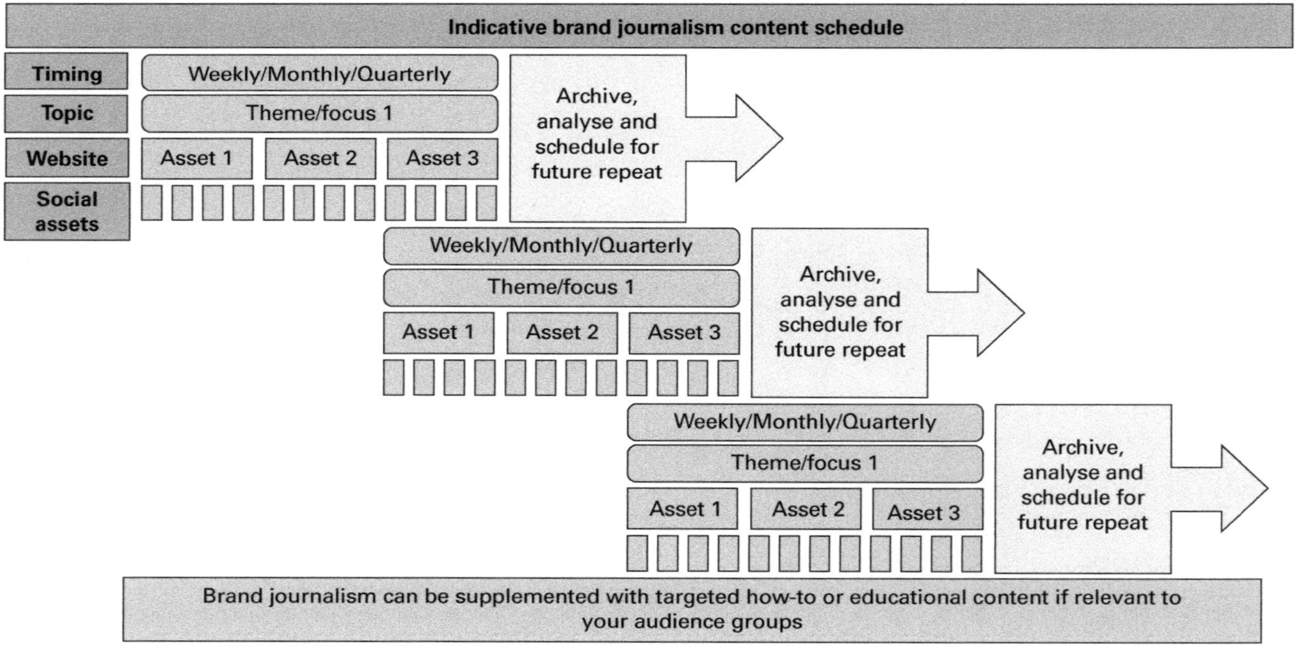

Indicative brand journalism content schedule

Timing	Weekly/Monthly/Quarterly	Weekly/Monthly/Quarterly	Weekly/Monthly/Quarterly
Topic	Theme/focus 1	Theme/focus 1	Theme/focus 1
Website	Asset 1	Asset 2	Asset 3	Asset 1	Asset 2	Asset 3	Asset 1	Asset 2	Asset 3
Social assets						

Archive, analyse and schedule for future repeat

Archive, analyse and schedule for future repeat

Archive, analyse and schedule for future repeat

Brand journalism can be supplemented with targeted how-to or educational content if relevant to your audience groups

Ultimately you don't necessarily know, and you don't necessarily have the control that says, 'I'm going to plant this seed, and it will grow right now, right here'. That seed may get taken and planted somewhere else; it may blow in the wind; it might grow to be something completely different. But if you're not sowing seeds, you'll never get anything growing. Yes, you are taking a risk in producing content, but it's not a risk that's unmanageable, and it's for a payback that is potentially very, very long term. We've now been doing this for five or six years, and we've got evergreen stories that we published right at the start that still deliver audiences and still speak to people. Good, relevant content is a gift that keeps on giving.

Campaign content

One-off campaign content will build peaks into your regular cadence and rhythm of publication and can target specific audiences. This type of content can be developed based on your marketing or PR activities, or broader industry or organizational timelines, for instance:

- Build campaign content around product launches or PR events, ensuring you get maximum amplification for your stories.
- Create campaigns around key people moves, for instance a new CEO or senior-level executive switching roles.
- Use the broader calendar of external events to drive a campaign – for example, Pride Week.
- Use an internal event to support your timing – for instance an internal conference or supplier/vendor event.
- If you have a specific product you are promoting or launching into a region or market then use this to support a campaign.
- Market creation can be supported by targeted campaign material that rolls out alongside your ongoing content.

For software company Red Hat, the Global Director of Content Laura Hamlyn explained to me that she has evolved the approach to content commissioning to always reflect the needs of the customer – campaign content ebbs and flows, reflecting specific customer pain points, whilst evergreen content maintains audience levels:

> We believe evergreen content and campaign content can work together well. For example, organic traffic to our website actually converts over time and creates some of our most valuable leads.

> Our teams have aligned to messaging via what we call 'sales conversations'. These are themes we identified via research that our customers and prospects have identified as challenges/opportunities for their business. We align with these themes across all of our marketing teams so sales, marketing, and our prospects and customers are all exposed to the same terms and concepts.

> Evergreen content builds trust, educates, and becomes a reliable source of information from day to day or month to month. Campaign content is more dynamic and fluid and can serve to create brand awareness via paid media, or function as a call to action telling the prospect what action to take next. As our data and MarTech get more advanced, we can personalize any of this content dynamically to reflect our customer and prospect goals and user profiles.

Develop a commissioning process

As we have already seen, your content rhythm, format, delivery, and amplification aspirations will always be driven by your available budget and resources.

If your budget is extremely limited, you will need to assess what types of content you can create most cost-effectively, and how you can get maximum value from them. If you are lucky, it may also be possible to find internal partners (and their budgets) who are willing to support your content aspirations, for instance in sales, communications or other areas of marketing support. Generally speaking though, there are three main options for approaching your content production:

TABLE 3.2 Content sourcing options

In-house content production	Many larger brands (especially in B2C) have taken their content production and creation in-house. This can assist in maintaining strong lines of control, but the associated longer-term commitment to headcount can be unappealing for some organizations.
Part in-house production – part agency or freelance	Keep some of your content in-house – ideally commissioning and editing – and outsource some tasks on the value chain such as content production and creation.
Fully outsourced model	Establish one provider as your content strategist and content producer, or build a network of agencies or providers who can support all aspects of the content supply chain.

Managing the flow of content in your organization requires having one overseeing department or editor. This unit, person or department will manage the editorial flow of content and ensure themes are coordinated to target audiences or personas. Using a hub and spoke structure allows a centralized editorial vision to be held and driven in one department – or potentially individual – with commissioning or content creation devolved to internal teams or external agencies. A devolved model will see responsibility for content creation and distribution to local or regional divisions and/or marketing teams.

System governance

Whatever your content format, and however regularly it is created, you will need to establish a system for analysing, guiding and reviewing it – either individually in detail, or as a whole. If you are a highly networked organization, the simplest and most effective way to build governance into your approach is to establish an Editorial Board or Content Advisory Group (CAG), either a real or virtual network. Your CAG should include representatives from marketing strategy, communications/PR, sales and relevant wider divisions who can take an active hand in guiding the following:

Marketing and PR integration: are you fully integrated and aware of activity in the wider marketing and PR teams? Is there a regular flow of material and information from your team to theirs (or vice versa) to enable calendars and campaigns to be coordinated?

Partnerships and stakeholders: are you connecting with all relevant areas of the business to include their thinking and stories into the narrative flow? Often, sustaining the flow of content from around the organization is the biggest challenge, especially for larger multinationals. Selling in your vision and building a team of evangelists through internal stakeholders will support the wider aspirations you have for your brand journalism.

Sales coordination: is your content reaching your sales teams and is it useful or relevant to them in their conversations with potential customers? It's not about using content marketing as pure sales collateral but using it to open doors for potential discussions.

Measurement and data: can you measure what you're doing? Bring in a wider cohort of people to review and discuss content and to supply information and success metrics that can support your ROI and discussions around success.

Establishing what you want to achieve with your content – and how you will deliver on those aims – is just a starting point. Once the strategy is mapped out, the key to efficient ongoing delivery is a resourcing plan and a management structure that will allow you, your team, or your agency to deliver consistent brand journalism content as a regular flow. Refining and reviewing your approach consistently based on success data and metrics will enable you to remain agile and responsive in what is a constantly changing marketing environment.

Notes

1 Prophet (2018) There are 5 content strategy archetypes – pick one, *Prophet*, 12 July. Available from: https://www.prophet.com/2018/07/choosing-the-right-content-strategy-archetype/ (archived at https://perma.cc/T9UW-TBLJ)

2 Dun & Bradsheet (nd) Perspectives. Available from: https://www.dnb.co.uk/perspectives.html

3 American Express (nd) Business Trends and Insights, American Express. Available from: https://www.americanexpress.com/en-gb/business/trends-and-insights/ (archived at https://perma.cc/CPJ6-5C2M)

4 Prophet (2018) The 2018 state of digital content, *Prophet*. Available from: https://insights.prophet.com/2018-state-of-digital-content (archived at https://perma.cc/35SH-KFFQ)

5 Demand Gen Report (2019) 2019 Content Preferences Survey: Growing demand for credible and concise content reinforces need for research and relevancy in B2B messaging, *Demand Gen Report*, Hasbrouck Heights, NJ. Available from: https://www.demandgenreport.com/resources/reports/2019-content-preferences-survey-report (archived at https://perma.cc/J5EW-CMBJ)

6 The One Brief (nd) Available from: https://theonebrief.com/ (archived at https://perma.cc/SJ9Q-LNDY)

7 i-cio (nd) Global Intelligence for the CIO. Available from: https://www.i-cio.com/ (archived at https://perma.cc/7NRW-EDNL)

8 The Future of Engagement and Commerce (nd) Available from: https://www.the-future-of-commerce.com/ (archived at https://perma.cc/DZN8-SZ7U)

9 Mailchimp (nd) Voice and Tone, Mailchimp Content Style Guide. Available from: https://styleguide.mailchimp.com/voice-and-tone/ (archived at https://perma.cc/C44K-83UC)

10 Silber, T (2018) Multinational conglomerate GE Goes all in on content marketing, *Forbes*, 20 June. Available from: https://www.forbes.com/sites/tonysilber/2018/06/20/multinational-conglomerate-ge-goes-all-in-on-content-marketing/#9ad774963da3 (archived at https://perma.cc/43KG-WR5L)

04

Finding the narrative: telling the stories that matter

Sourcing stories with impact

The days of a simple B2B buying journey are long behind us. Today future buyers are influenced by a wider range of content than ever before, from an increasingly wide range of sources. The process is more complex, more layered and ultimately much more long-winded.

Because of this, your brand has to stand out from the crowd and the stories your brand tells must reflect the essence of what that brand stands for. And because everything you say and everything you do interconnects as part of both your brand identity and your overarching narrative, it's important to be clear on your narrative from the start.

Overcoming corporate myopia

The most common trap organizations fall into is believing their audiences will be interested in every announcement they make, or that any news event, or any new piece of information is good enough. Corporate myopia tends to lead organizations to produce sub-standard, bland content that does them no favours at all. News output and announcements have merit and resonance as part of your marketing and communications mix, but won't develop or grow long-term relationships with audiences.

To get a sense of what you need to do to change this, you only need to ask yourself how much time you spend each day being meaningfully engaged with content produced by other organizations. It could be a video on LinkedIn or something you've been emailed. What is it that makes you stop what you're doing and pay attention? What does it take for you to arrest the scroll and click through and sign up to a newsletter, for instance? Think along these lines to get yourself into the mindset of applying the right narrative to your content.

What makes a great B2B story?

We've said already that great content is about creating great stories. But the narrative tropes and storytelling arcs that so often feature in 'how to write a story' blogs/books might not always translate well into the B2B environment. There are a range of approaches you might take to structuring and telling your brand stories to encourage audiences to stay with you and your content.

Chip and Dan Heath address this point in their book *Made to Stick: Why some ideas survive and others die.*[1] The brothers propose six applicable principles that they believe make ideas as a whole more 'sticky'.

Principle	What does that mean in practice?	For your B2B Content
Simplicity	Relentlessly prioritize and strip out the extraneous to ensure your idea sticks.	Stick to one idea, one thought – what's the one point you are trying to make with this piece?
Unexpectedness	'Violate people's expectations' to gain attention.	Find nuances, personalities, analogies or case studies that will pique the audiences' attention to explain or elaborate.
Concreteness	Explain your ideas in human actions, with real examples or concrete imagery.	Bring your content to life with case studies, real people, real life examples, comparisons or word pictures.

(continued)

(Continued)

Principle	What does that mean in practice?	For your B2B Content
Credibility	'Sticky ideas have to carry their own credentials' – this makes people believe.	Add credentials, quote an expert, or give a tangible example or case study; use real life examples, numbers or reference points where you can.
Emotions	Make the audience feel something – an emotional idea makes people care.	Engage with a human tale, a tale of good v bad, the challenge of unpicking a problem that was insurmountable.
Stories	Help us act, by demonstrating and inspiring us.	Build a strong narrative, or clear structure to deliver powerful messages in a world swamped with content.

These principles can be applied to B2B content you produce for your organization, and they work especially well for narrative blogs, videos and articles that might form the basis of your content hub or blog site. Integrate what you can of these principles to help your stories arrest the scroll and gain the attention of your audiences.

Building a message framework

Before you can create anything you need to be clear about your communications messages. A simple messaging framework can guide and support your content if you are not clear what you should be talking about and what subjects should form the core of your content. It will also help you clarify your messages and how you should talk about your organization.

While some businesses will have multiple communications frameworks for different sectors, divisions and areas, a small business might only have one messaging or communications approach. Ultimately though, a narrative framework doesn't have to be overly complicated – it just needs to encapsulate the core offer and supporting messages and points.

FIGURE 4.1 A messaging framework

Our mission narrative	We support our customers with **[this activity]**, that offers **[these benefits to our customers]** in order that they can **[achieve these goals]**			
Communications themes	How we achieve our mission 1	How we achieve our mission 2	How we achieve our mission 3	
	Underpinned by [this]			
	AND Underpinned by [this]			
Communications messages	Supporting message 1		Supporting message 2	
Proof points / reasons to believe	Proof points: area or example 1	Proof points: area or example 2	Proof points: area or example 3	Proof points: area or example 4

If you need to develop one for your organization, start with the overarching mission and build your framework from there.

Your messaging framework should include these core pieces of information:

- **The mission or narrative:** this is the main or overarching message or mission of your organization, or potentially your business unit, geography or division. Your headline messaging outlines the total business offer and could also include the outcomes you drive for customers.

- **Communications themes:** a handful of communications themes will underpin your primary narrative. These will summarize the thrust of your business and what makes your offer appealing and unique. You could have between three and five specific messages, supported by core principles or behaviours, or cultural assets that underpin this activity.

- **Communications messages:** these will be messages distilled from your narrative and themes that you might use in publicity material, speeches or primers for your key people as spokespeople or for PR appearances.

- **Proof points:** these are the examples, 'reasons to believe', case studies, stories and people that support your messaging. They demonstrate what you are doing in real life and can form the basis of some of your storytelling. You could also categorize according to your client or customer 'pain points', taking as the start of your content development the issues that are challenging your audience base.

Which stories should your organization create?

It's all very well saying content must travel through your broader network and your target micro-networks without friction, that it must interest people organically – but what does this actually mean?

Ultimately, all content should have value. Sites such as the *D!gitalist*,[2] created by SAP, offer stories of insight and value that tap into a range of different topics – from the overarching challenges of a changing world, to the specific work being done by CIOs and CFOs (stories such as the '25 Most Important Customer Experience Questions Answered'[3]). Hewlett Packard Enterprise's Community hub,[4] meanwhile, offers technically led content, as well as tapping into the wider challenges of the modern IT professional (stories include titles such as 'Why DevOps fails!').

Building awareness with stories of value

Not all content is working for the same results, and stories will need to deliver different insight and messaging – and encourage different actions or responses – depending on where in the sales funnel they sit.

Brand journalism is about bringing in, and engaging with, a B2B audience *before* targets and audiences have entered the notional sales funnel and are only just embarking on their customer journey. Your task is to develop stories that engage audiences by delivering insight or information that aligns with their values to start conversations and relationships with target buyers (and the networks of target buyers) before there is a demonstrated need. By understanding your audience and creating broad content that reflects the world around them and their own concerns and challenges, you will catch their attention, you will build interest and influence how your brand is viewed. At the pre-funnel stage your stories will ideally be broad in scope with limited brand reference, reflecting the world we live in today.

The case for broad content

Don't be afraid to develop more wide-ranging 'raincatcher' content. Broad and contextual stories reflect the issues, narratives and challenges of the world we live in, and it's a world that brands also operate in. As such, these stories should be created to attract the attention of our audiences and pull them in.

However, the stories – told in whatever format – must reflect the values and beliefs of your target audience and must resonate with the themes and insights they are discussing in their everyday life and work. As Amy Hatch, former global head of content marketing for SAP Customer Experience, explains in an interview for this book, it's crucial to see your audience as *people* first, and B2B *buyers* second:

FIGURE 4.2   Raincatcher content: engaging audiences before the start of the sales funnel

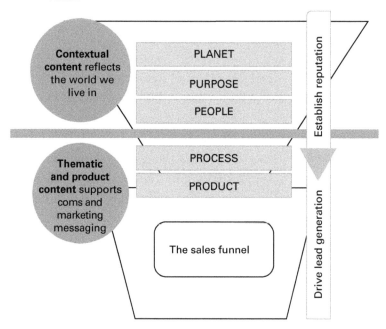

The audience is the very foundation of our strategy – that is audience first, and not even customer. It's empathy for the reader, empathy for what they're going through, understanding their world, and understanding that there's constant change that's vital. The pace of change in history is more rapid now than ever before, and that affects everybody from every piece, and every part of their world. The point is, when people go to work, they're not suddenly a different person. They're still the same person who watches Netflix, who tweets, who looks at Facebook, who sends an email, and so we approach our content creation with that hat on. There is no such thing as a B2B person. You don't go to work and become a B2B person. I want to be engaged the same way I am when I'm reading a parenting blog as when I'm reading about content marketing.

If you understand the context clearly – the world we live in, the challenges business and individuals face, the existential narrative of our world and the people in it – you will be better equipped to create stories that are both relevant and meaningful and that will travel efficiently through networks.

Finding stories that resonate

Broadly speaking, it is useful to divide contextual content into the following story groupings:

PLANET	The world we live in, what is challenging or informing us. New trends and issues that influence the world around us, our lives and our work.
PURPOSE	Trends in the way we work and run businesses; how companies and countries are led; the importance of values; the nature of leadership.
PEOPLE	Stories of individuals or leaders, evangelists or thought leaders in an organization. This could be their personal story, or insight, their guidance or advice on relevant topics.
PROCESS	Industry and business stories, information and insight on the broader topics in the sector of interest for your organization.
PRODUCT	Your priority narratives to drive business growth through sales of your products and services.

Each story grouping has its own relevance for particular pieces of content, so it's worth looking at each of them in more detail.

Planet: Researching the conversation ecosystem

Put simply, planet-based content tackles and reflects the broader conversations that your audiences and customers are having about the world around them. It's therefore essential that you and your writing teams are plugged into the macro insights and trends that are shaping the broader social context, the wider news agenda and world events and narratives.

Groundbreaking content is that which creates intelligent stories that resonate at this level and are predicated on having a clear understanding of the context in which your organization is operating. At this stage you could map a broad cross-section of themes and trends, rather than those that are directly impacting your work.

The World Economic Forum's content is a good example of this type of brand journalism. Stories on its *Agenda*[5] site are broad and topical. The Forum has consistently tapped into the *zeitgeist*, the key discussions, the obsessions, the mythologies and concerns of the wider populace, and does it by seeking the views of business, academics and thought leaders. Not only has it told these stories effectively, it has found new formats and new approaches to deliver these narratives. World Economic Forum content has been shared many millions of times and has supported the Forum in driving huge growth in follower numbers, as well as shifting perception of the brand. At times it has also had a practical impact on communities, as World Economic Forum Managing Director Adrian Monck explained to me:

> Stories that work for us are those that leave people with a sense of optimism and hope about complicated and big topics. Take a subject like climate change – that's on everyone's mind. Can we give people information that says, 'There's something you can do, the situation is not hopeless'? The most important thing about content is motivating

people to act or challenging apathy. For me, finding stories that give people an example of what can be done, that inspire action, and also help create connections is crucial.

Purpose: Leading with your values

As we saw in Chapter 1, trust in our established political and societal leaders has diminished, and individuals are looking for new role models.

People are turning to leaders of companies to demonstrate how to 'do the right thing' in the absence of national governments taking action on issues they are concerned about. As the Edelman Trust Barometer[6] for 2019 outlined, more than three-quarters of people surveyed believe company leaders should proactively take the lead on emerging social and environmental issues rather than waiting for governments to take action. In addition, 71 per cent of employees said they believe it's important for their CEO to respond to current societal and global challenges – for instance political events, employee-related issues and industry events.

This creates a huge opportunity for creating authentic, purpose-based content. It's an opportunity for brands to stand up for what they believe in and to proclaim their real, genuine purpose. It's an opportunity to reflect brand values, aligning yourselves with the values of your audience and those you want to influence.

Here's Marc Benioff, CEO of Salesforce.com, with his wider view on what business can do to drive change:

> It's my belief that businesses are the greatest platforms for change and can have an enormous impact on improving the state of the world. As business leaders we are in positions of influence, and responsible for more than just shareholders. We are accountable for the wellbeing of an extended community of employees, customers and partners, as well as our fellow beings on this planet we inhabit.[7]

There are many examples of companies starting to demonstrate and write about their strongly held beliefs, on society, for instance, or other issues where they might have impact, such as technology companies discussing the impact of automation.

CASE STUDY ARTICLE

Four ways to help close the skills gap in the age of automation: Autodesk[8]

With this article, and with others on the *Redshift* site, Autodesk demonstrates a commitment to its avowed commitment: 'At Autodesk, we're focused on how we can help both businesses and workers succeed and thrive in the age of automation.'

CASE STUDY SITE

i-CIO.com: Fujitsu[9]

Some organizations choose to align themselves to a particular topic by creating a space where issues can be discussed, albeit not always authored by their own senior people. The *i-cio.com* site created by Fujitsu hosts 'big thinkers' on the site who create or author content that challenges conventional thinking and/or tackles some of the issues facing the world today.

Many larger organizations have the size, impact and customer base that allows them to discuss these types of topics widely, with no negative impact. That is not the case for all companies and in all countries, who might not be able to talk openly and freely about, for instance, representation and equality, due to societal or governmental constraints. Consider carefully how you and your company approach complex or controversial topics; align your messaging clearly with that emanating from your communications and corporate communications teams.

CASE STUDY EXAMPLE

Gay rights failures holding back Asian banking: Bloomberg[10]

Hosted on Bloomberg's own *Insights* hub, this piece is just one of a range of articles that tackle inequality in the workplace for LGBTQ workers, the disabled and other minorities. The site header states: 'As our global client base becomes increasingly diverse, our focus on diversity and inclusion helps us stay attuned to our clients' rich and varied cultures, norms and business practices.'[11]

People: Demonstrating your human side

Personal viewpoints and testimonies are a powerful way of approaching your content. When done well, they're authentic, engaging and informative. The power of one person's unedited view – especially if that person holds a senior position at a large organization – is not to be underestimated.

Broadly speaking, 'personal' stories will often be categorized as *thought leadership*, which I cover in more detail in Chapter 10. Thought leaders are innovative, forward thinkers who can create content so good that it engages broad audiences and is shared widely. They can theoretically come from any level in your organization, but authority tends to increase with experience, although not always seniority.

In terms of the kinds of personal brand journalism content that these thought leaders should look to share, the most powerful are those that reflect the concerns or interests of the broad audience you are trying to build brand awareness with. There are many thought leaders/influencers in B2B who are also writing on highly technical topics (both on their own sites, blogs and on other specific sites such as Reddit or through WhatsApp groups).

CASE STUDY EXAMPLE

Will a smarter social safety net help people survive the Age of Automation? Autodesk[12]

This article is written by the CEO of Autodesk, Andrew Anagnost, who argues that there is a responsibility for organizations and governments to take action to support those groups of people who may be negatively impacted by the continued rise of technology and automation. Dr Anagnost is an authentic CEO who chooses to speak his mind on multiple topics on the Autodesk content hub, *Redshift*.

It's worth noting the personal can also overlap with the product and the process, or the purpose of the business to cover a wide range of subject areas, for instance:

- **Educating:** education and new insights on broader management, leadership or operational challenges.
- **Campaigning:** responding to the challenges or conundrums facing the broader industry – the *What should we do?* or *What needs to happen?*
- **Sharing:** insights and inspiration from that person's experience and track record – the *What do they think?* and *What would they do?*
- **Aggregating:** grouping other people's thoughts together, or those of their team, to shape an argument or point of view.

Process: Researching your business or industry environment

With a clear understanding of the broader environment that frames the conversations of potential audiences and customers, you can start to focus on finding specific narratives/stories that are relevant to your specific industry, business or sector. If you are looking for a starting point for these stories, consider thinking about story ideas under these broad headings:

INNOVATION	SUCCESS	TRENDS	CHALLENGES	EVENTS
What's coming down the track? What's new and innovative and what might the future hold?	What examples can you discuss from your organization or beyond that demonstrate success with a particular challenge?	What are the trends that are shaping the future of your sector, industry or organization? How are you responding and what does that mean for your customers, or society?	What is keeping your customers or audiences awake at night? Can you start to discuss these issues or concerns?	What are you learning from the events in your sector? What are industry experts discussing?

INNOVATION STORY EXAMPLE
The rise of the humble brown box: MHI[13]

Taking as its starting point the increasing demand for boxes for online shopping product delivery, this piece tracks the history of the cardboard box, and new engineering techniques shaping its development (driven by Mitsubishi Heavy Industries). Build a story such as this from one simple statistic – in this case the predicted growth in the brown box industry.

The content hub *Redshift* has been created by software developers Autodesk.[14] The site content covers how products, buildings and cities will be built in the future. It's broad and reads like a magazine. Head of Content Distribution and Social Media at Autodesk, Luke Kintigh, explained the approach to this brand journalism site:

> At *Redshift* we basically have a full-blown newsroom inside the company. We produce content much like a magazine. Our primary outcome is to build the brand and to shift perception from a brand that simply produces AutoCAD to a company that provides a wider range of software to a range of businesses. We're not a product blog; we focus on the people and not the product. Part of the strategy is to cover multiple industries and provide value to our audiences – for instance around how the way things are changing could be applied to how you design a shoe or to how you design a skyscraper. We have some amazing people in the company driving change and getting their perspective and point of view is at the heart of our strategy. But we also include other sources, sometimes partners and customers who can tell the full story of, for instance, how Autodesk is helping with product design, but also what's it like to see a project come to fruition.

TRENDS STORY EXAMPLE
Six ways AI improves daily life: SAP[15]

On the *D!gitalist* content hub from SAP, this simple listicle takes as its starting point the impact that artificial intelligence is having on our daily lives. It's straightforward and written for a broad audience in non-technical language. Use this type of piece as a jumping-off point for more detailed content if required.

Product: Your business making a difference

Although a key tenet of brand journalism is *not* to push products, it is still possible to develop thoughtful product-related material that has brand journalism characteristics to ensure it is more popular, more shared or more engaging.

To do so, you must map out the kinds of questions that your audience(s) might have when thinking about purchasing your product or service and work backwards from there to develop lists of potential titles and subject areas.

Narrative approaches can often be developed in bulk for this type of content, and so ideally you would set up formats or approaches that allow this content to be easily and quickly prepared and uploaded (see Chapter 6 for more ideas on what formats you should choose). Examples of this type of content could include:

- **Case study-led problem solving content:** using examples of specific issues or wider problems that have been solved by your product. Frame your product as the 'hero'.

- **Explainers:** 'What is...' content explains a product approach, a concept or a business solution, while 'How to...' content gives advice and guidance on common challenges or areas of business they might be tackling. There's also 'What's the benefit of...' content that tackles different approaches to various challenges, while 'About us...' content can dip into how the culture of the business impacts outputs, products and solutions.

- **Thought leadership:** thought starters, overviews and commentary from key thinkers and managers can touch upon products as specific solutions for broader problems.

- **Profiles:** who are your people, what do they know, what's their experience and what insight do they have about this product or service? *Forecast* is a site created and hosted by enterprise software company Nutanix and promises to explore ideas and technologies that are shaping our future. Edited by Ken Kaplan, it has an entire section dedicated to the 'profiles' of Nutanix people. These people have a story to tell that feeds directly back into the work of the company.

Don't forget 'the brand'

How much is too much?

You can follow all the content marketing models you want, but there's one question many brand journalists often get stuck on: how much should they reference the brand?

The hubs and content I am focusing on as brand journalism content are light on brand mentions and instead focus on adding insight and encouraging sharing, primarily because they're interesting stories. Many of the sites and publications referenced here mention the brand very little, and are looking to develop brand awareness through telling stories of value – for instance SAP's *FCEC* and Roland Berger's

Think:Act publication. By sharing the content as insight they hope to engage a target audience and build engagement at a later date. Other sites will mention their brand less in the copy, but will have links to further branded suggested reading.

The benefits of 'low' or 'no' brand reference

Companies that have a long-term vision to grow a robust and authentic audience for their content might decide not to mention the brand at all or only mention it tangentially.

By shifting focus away from the brand, marketers and communicators are less tempted to foist their own brand message on to their audience, ensuring they are more focused on the needs of the buyer. As marketing thought leader Heidi Taylor writes:

> …we need to create content, tell stories and have conversations that are not about the products or services we sell, but about the big issues that are really important and personal to our customers. It's these issues that bring the human element to what we do, make conversations more meaningful and build relationships that last, enabling us to engage with our customers in ways that will linger in their hearts and minds long after any sales promotion or marketing campaign is over.[18]

One downside to this strategy is that a longer-term approach can be challenging to sell to more short-cycle marketing leaders. Here, you need to make the case that it can take time to develop an audience (especially if you have limited access to paid amplification), but that it will pay off in the longer term, particularly when long-tail audiences build from archive content amplification. Also, any content created can be stretched further as the basis of lead generation and demand generation activity further down the sales funnel (for instance, built out to an e-book or gated white paper).

On SAP's *Future of Customer Engagement and Commerce* site, the content hub is branded, but only lightly so. None of the stories on the site include brand referencing. This was a conscious decision by the SAP team when the site launched. The brand sits only on the site as a logo and on the banner, and on the bottom navigation, along with right-hand navigation links and click-throughs.

Whichever path you take for your narrative structure, you will need a system in place to ensure that you can continue to deliver on your brand journalism promises. That means making sure that you have a process to source and deliver content in whatever guise or format. We will cover production in later chapters, but many organizations find that the toughest challenge is to source engaging stories from their everyday activities – and this is where thinking like a journalist can help from the start.

Notes

1   Heath, C and Heath, D (2008) *Made to Stick: Why some ideas take hold and others die*, Random House, pp 15–19

2   D!gitalist Magazine (nd). Available from: https://www.digitalistmag.com/ (archived at https://perma.cc/Y5PE-K3UE)

3   Koch, C (2015) The 25 most important customer experience questions answered, *D!gitalist*, 18 February. Available from: https://www.digitalistmag. com/lob/sales-marketing/2015/02/18/25-important-customer-experience-questions-answered-02253418 (archived at https://perma.cc/TB37-XVU7)

4   Hewlett Packard Enterprise Community (nd). Available from: https:// community.hpe.com/ (archived at https://perma.cc/9N6L-RPSF)

5   World Economic Forum (nd). Available from: http://weforum.org/agenda (archived at https://perma.cc/AZA6-33CD)

6   Edelman (2019) 2019 Edelman Trust Barometer: Expectations for CEOs, *Edelman*, 29 April. Available from: https://www.edelman.com/research/ trust-barometer-expectations-for-ceos-2019 (archived at https://perma.cc/ LAX4-U6ZV)

7   Benioff, M (2016) Businesses are the greatest platforms for change, *Huffpost*, 18 January. Available from: https://www.huffpost.com/entry/businesses-are-the-great_b_8993240 (archived at https://perma.cc/4N5P-KDJL)

8   Speicher, J (2019) Four ways to help close the skills gap in the age of automation, *Autodesk*, 12 June. Available from: https://adsknews.autodesk. com/views/four-ways-to-close-the-skills-gap-in-the-age-of-automation (archived at https://perma.cc/GX5P-7J9V)

9   Ritchie, R (2019) Defining a new ethic for technology, *I by Global Intelligence for the CIO*, May. Available from: https://www.i-cio.com/management/insight/ item/a-new-ethic-for-technology (archived at https://perma.cc/J6SH-PAJV)

10 Gopalan, N (2019) Gay rights failures are holding back Asia banking, *Bloomberg*, 6 May. Available from: https://www.bloomberg.com/diversity-inclusion/blog/gay-rights-failures-holding-back-asia-banking/ (archived at https://perma.cc/S962-J7C8)

11 Bloomberg (nd) Activating every employee's potential, *Bloomberg*. Available from: https://www.bloomberg.com/diversity-inclusion (archived at https://perma.cc/2E4E-PCTY)

12 Anagnost, A (2019) Will a smarter social safety net help people survive the age of automation? *Redshift by Autodesk*, 12 June. Available from:https://www.autodesk.com/redshift/age-of-automation/ (archived at https://perma.cc/K96J-7DU9)

13 Jezard, A (2018) The rise of the humble brown box, *Spectra*, 15 November. Available from: https://spectra.mhi.com/the-rise-of-the-humble-brown-box (archived at https://perma.cc/32VM-T5MJ)

14 Redshift by Autodesk (nd). Available from: https://www.autodesk.com/redshift/ (archived at https://perma.cc/JAY2-SB28)

15 Gardner, K (2019) Six ways AI improves daily life, *D!gitalist Magazine*, 18 May. Available from: https://www.digitalistmag.com/improving-lives/2019/05/28/6-ways-ai-improves-daily-life-06198539 (archived at https://perma.cc/N24G-YK2X

16 Hynes, C (2019) From college campuses to sports stadiums, IoT may hold the key to public safety, *Dell Technologies*, 12 June. Available from: https://www.delltechnologies.com/en-us/perspectives/from-college-campuses-to-sports-stadiums-iot-may-hold-the-key-to-public-safety/ (archived at https://perma.cc/KM46-C92S)

17 Centrica (nd) How algorithms deliver renewables to the grid, *Centrica Platform*. Available from: https://www.centrica.com/platform/ai-renewables (archived at https://perma.cc/68RK-8J95)

18 Taylor, H (2017) *B2B Marketing Strategy: Differentiate, develop and deliver lasting customer engagement*, Kogan Page Publishers, p 17

05

Story mining: uncovering your powerful brand journalism

Even the best stories can't tell themselves. Committing to creating a regular flow of content means also committing time and resources to the vital job of someone (or some mechanism) producing it and getting it out for public consumption. At first this can feel like a daunting task: it means creating an efficient process for finding, producing, and publishing content.

Brand journalism is not about creating PR stories that you can place in publications (media relations) and nor is it about developing examples of where you have been successful with client work (case studies). It is about taking your expertise and knowledge and creating stories that align your brand with a particular way of thinking by either delivering a portion of that knowledge, or insight that will help to develop your audience capabilities.

> Story mining is a process that enables you to integrate *longevity* and *relevance* to your content.

Establishing your process

Whilst every company is different, and the content it produces will clearly be unique to itself, it shouldn't matter whether you're planning a technical white paper, an explainer video, or a social campaign – the

FIGURE 5.1 The story-mining process

IDEATION	PLANNING	SIGN-OFF
Editorial team agrees key themes Integrate internal messaging and priorities Source ideas from network Schedule ongoing story workshops Develop ideas submission system	Brainstorm long list ideas Review against aims and calendar Map and confirm ideas, dates and schedule Integrate review system for submitted ideas Schedule ongoing brainstorming	Develop titles for agreed stories, as well as source Create approx. 100-word abstracts for agreed stories Sign off and commission stories/ content items

mechanics of creating content are the same. Everything needs to be aligned to your business on some level, and it must deliver on a specific aim or purpose.

Story mining involves developing mechanisms and processes to surface information-rich stories from all parts of the organization or its network that can be developed into multiple formats within your content schedule.

Building a flow of stories

Establishing a system is key to maintaining the flow of ideas within your organization. Longevity is really about sustainability of stories. For most large companies, finding a few short-term (one-off), internal stories is relatively easy. What's more tricky is finding relevant ideas on an ongoing basis to create a sustained flow of stories.

Establishing a system adhering to certain criteria and processes will ensure you identify and create stories that align with your business ethos and needs, demonstrate your thought leadership skills, and create a platform to display your credentials and proof points. At its simplest, good story mining becomes a process for identifying the right stories from within your organization – those which your target audiences will find appealing, relatable, and which will help you and your organization meet its business objectives.

In Chapter 3 I described some of the tenets of brand journalism, and in Chapter 4 I discussed how to find the narrative – this chapter will tackle the challenge of keeping the ideas coming, generating an atmosphere of creativity and finding those stories in all parts of the business.

A broad approach to finding narratives

It's worth reinforcing at this point that you need to agree and share with others the types of stories you are looking for in the first place.

The *Raincatcher* model outlined in the previous chapter explains an approach to creating stories of interest related to your corporate environment that can be created by your content teams and distributed across multiple channels. These are briefly summarized here:

Planet	Purpose	People	Process	Product
These are the issues challenging the planet. You can put your own corporate prism on these narratives, delivering a clear sense of your value set.	Use stories to give a true sense of the values of your organization. Buyers want to understand what your organization's position is on the most challenging topics of our time.	These are the human stories you can tell that reflect how your organization operates. They are the people that make your company tick.	These stories tap into the wider business environment and themes within it. They are broad topics, tangentially aligned to your industry or product.	Product stories tell of a challenge where a product or service is the hero. Ensure the value or benefit is upfront and at the top of your story, not the specification.

The wider story environment

Try to understand the types of stories that the wider populace is hearing and sharing. Globally, for instance, a trend towards an increase in diversity in many countries is broadly welcomed.[1] There are other stories that are challenging traditional belief systems, such as those that focus on equality, environmental challenges or the impact of artificial intelligence and computing on the traditional workplace.

Other, world-based issues that suit statistical analysis or trends-based commentary include our ageing populations, our growing population, and a migration to urban areas from the countryside. If we understand the broader context of these discussions and concerns, we can become more relevant with our storytelling.

The sources you choose will undoubtedly be influenced by the world view of organizations that are publishing them, but there is a wealth of material from which to draw. You can turn to publications such as the World Economic Forum's *Agenda*[2] website, mentioned previously, or pull on global publications that you know and trust, or national and international newspapers.

As well as reading relevant publications and literature, also take note of the mountains of research and insight, mostly freely available, that informs these discussions. Remember:

- Wider trend stories will give audiences a true sense of your organization's thinking and its way of working, enabling them to engage more completely in a conversation or relationship.
- These mega trends will inform broader, evergreen articles that might touch on wider challenges of running a business or organization.
- Global narratives will inform thought leadership and articles that guide on aspects of leadership, broad management or response to societal influences.
- Evergreen articles created with these themes in mind can be the broad base on which your company or organization builds its wider narrative and reputation.

Other sources include academics, research bodies and industry bodies. All give an insight into the key challenges faced by the world as a whole, and can inform areas you can move into, or have a view on.

Looking internally for ideas

Narratives that reflect the challenges of your industry and the benefits of your product can be surfaced using internal evangelists, communications teams and editorial team members. Other sources that can be leveraged and managed by your central editorial team include:

- **Agency writers and editorial teams.** If you are working with an agency you can challenge them to manage the story-mining process on your behalf, using their own people and network as well as regular workshops to surface additional ongoing ideas. Whilst not always integrated into internal business decisions, an external team can sometimes ensure a regular flow is maintained.

- **Communications team members.** As those people who own and drive communications for your organization – and often former journalists themselves – the PR and communications staff will be a great source of ideas for your brand journalism and are often at the heart of the editorial team. Ideally team members can be given story goals and targets to encourage a sense of creativity and innovation in thinking and production techniques.

- **Sales and marketing teams.** Sales teams are often a wealth of knowledge about the challenges and questions posed by buyers, while marketing teams will deliver research, analytics and have internal research divisions to surface additional information. Seek out subject matter experts and those people who are the story finders and storytellers to whom you can turn for more information.

- **Original research or aggregated research** by industry bodies, independent bodies, think tanks, charities, analysts and corporate bodies should be integrated into the cycle of research. Often these groups publish a range of information, reports and data. These might include bodies such as The Organization for Economic Co-operation and Development, The Royal Society, The King's Fund, management consultancies such as PwC, KPMG and Deloitte, as well as organizations such as the UN, the World Bank and the African Development Bank. Also don't ignore philanthropic organizations – the likes of Chatham House in the UK, or the Milken Institute and the Aspen Institute in the United States.

Establishing an effective system to mine and surface ongoing stories – particularly in a larger or dispersed organization – can still be a challenge, even with a structure or approach in place. Jim Cox, a former journalist and now VP of Communications at global logistics organization Agility, champions storytelling, but also understands its challenges, especially with a B2B audience. He says:

Unearthing great stories can still be hit and miss. Often there are internal business and political considerations that can stop stories in their tracks, or thrust them forward even though they might have limited interest to the audience. Sometimes we find out about great stories and narratives, but only *after* they've gone stale. We are also faced – occasionally – with persuading stakeholders that the reward for sharing information is greater than the risk.

What's heartening, Cox adds, is that when things are done right, there is generally an appreciative audience: 'Human stories tend to resonate well, as do 'How-tos' for smaller businesses trying to get into international trade or understand emerging markets.' He adds: 'Balanced explainers that simplify something complex and offer a framework for the customer audience to make informed judgements are also successful.'

Subscribe to as many industry newsletters and content hubs as you can to find other relevant and informative information. It's even worth subscribing to your competitors' content to ensure you know what they are saying too, and how you might frame your own messages differently alongside theirs.

THE BENEFITS OF THE 'NEWS MEETING'

All daily and weekly newsrooms tend to follow a similar routine or process. At the start of each editorial day or week, news editors and daily output editors have a meeting for all members of the team to discuss the ongoing stories of interest – what's happened, what's happening, what's going to change during the course of the day etc. This news meeting is the opportunity to shape the news agenda by suggesting stories that 'fit' the **purpose** of the newsroom's output (whether serious, tabloid, global, local). Stories might have been sourced by the journalists who have uncovered exclusives through interviews, contacts and news sense, or the news might be dominated by coverage of scheduled events that have been on the agenda for some time such as elections, protests or demonstrations. The most productive news meetings are those where there is lively engagement and conversation from the team. The same is true of your own internal news meetings for your story and content development. You need to engender a sense of purpose in your story generation – ie what type of story will 'fit' the organization or company and reflect the brand's profile and tone of voice.

Encouraging a story culture

The most obvious way of driving ongoing content from your organization is to talk to people, internally and externally. It sounds simple, but in reality, you will need to apply a process and approach to this to ensure you deliver regularly and to your schedule.

Ken Kaplan was executive editor at Intel's *iQ*, which was launched in 2012 as a tech culture news and social media site. At its height, *iQ* attracted over 3 million page views a month.[3] In 2018, Kaplan became Editor in Chief of the *Forecast*, a business and technology news site by enterprise software company Nutanix. The branded site features original articles, videos and audio podcast segments about the people and tech trends driving digital transformation. Interviewed for this book, he explained how he approached story development for the *iQ* site:

> When I started directing the editorial side at iQ, I wanted to create original journalistic content. We went out and talked to people then wrote stories or produced videos relevant to anyone interested in technology; that's been the vibe I've gone after for a long time, which is a journalistic approach to storytelling, driven by great interviews. I want to pull more humanity and emotional aspects from people working on the cutting edge of technology. The technical challenges they overcame and the technology they used are definitely part of the story, but I also want to know what it's like, after two weeks of hitting their head on the wall about a problem, what clicked? How did it feel when all of a sudden everything made sense? When you have really good stories they ladder up to a living brand story that the company is always refining, honing and adjusting. That brand story is really made up of many anecdotal pieces that can be crystallized into an impactful brand message.

By demonstrating success with published stories and content being shared widely, you will start to build a 'story culture' – but how else do you encourage a story creation rhythm within the wider organization?

REWARD: ESTABLISH QUOTAS AND KPIs

Try encouraging your communications teams and business units to come up with a minimum number of ideas per week/month. Teams can be split up either by geography, verticals, industries or client groups depending on your story requirements. Where possible, reward innovation and consistency of thinking. This should help to boost the number of ideas coming through.

DEMONSTRATE: PROMOTE SUCCESS

Success breeds success. Try developing and promoting stories that have proved to be successful on your internal platforms. If you can demonstrate success, others in your organization will want to emulate this by promoting stories of their own. Coach writers about how to develop stories and you'll find more will start to deliver ideas.

EDUCATE: SHARE INSIGHT

Develop a toolkit for how disparate teams can source and share stories. This toolkit could comprise a story *pro forma* or list the key questions that individuals should ask within their own areas or divisions to elicit ideas and suggestions. Use your editorial board or communications teams to share and disperse the toolkit as well as centralized, and local, examples of best practice.

GIVE RECOGNITION: PUBLISH AND PROMOTE

It's vital your internal audience stays engaged in the practice of story mining. Without it there is danger of a loss of momentum. Colleagues and partner networks need to understand why they should get on board with your efforts. So you might also want to consider formal or informal recognition, or using internal communications to publicly thank those individuals who have either delivered, or come up with, strong ideas that have made it through to publication.

Developing a structure to deliver ongoing ideas

It's also worth remembering that how you build your team for successful ongoing delivery will also depend on your size and structure as an organization. Here are some of the approaches you could take to ensure your story-mining system continues to deliver ongoing 'gold' to your output.

TABLE 5.1 Four different approaches to story mining

Devolved hub-and-spoke model	<ul><li>Develop templates and questions to drive story sourcing.</li><li>Find evangelists in each business unit, sector or region.</li><li>Develop a sample story with an outline of what makes it great.</li><li>Suggest questions that evangelists can ask to source ideas and stories.</li><li>Create a template to share with co-workers in the field; this might even be developed as a 'toolkit' that explains what a good story looks like and what you require each story to contain.</li></ul>
Centralized model	<ul><li>One centralized communications/marketing team or staff member establishes all aspects of the content commissioning and production process, including communication objectives, calendar and required pattern and flow of story upload.</li><li>The centralized team undertakes its own story-mining sessions or interviews to develop content. Content might reflect local markets through interviews or desk research. Generic stories can have localized sections dropped in by regional business units, offices or operations.</li><li>Ideas are uploaded to a centralized document or online hub for consideration and sign-off.</li><li>Interviews or source information are sought from local representatives and stories are created centrally or outsourced.</li><li>One global management consultancy has no formal story surfacing structure or process; instead, each relevant division of the organization (eg energy, digital, financial services) is expected to surface and deliver its own ideas which are then reviewed and written by a central team of journalists.</li></ul>
Collaborative model	<ul><li>Establish a rhythm for face-to-face or remote group story ideation sessions. It could be six-monthly, quarterly, monthly, weekly, or (in some instances) daily, depending on corporate pressures, timelines and volumes of material required.</li><li>Facilitate face-to-face sessions using structured process for story generation. Sessions are led by communications or marketing team representatives.</li></ul>

(continued)

TABLE 5.1 (Continued)

Outsourced model	• Recruit an agency to develop story ideas, manage the process of story sourcing and mining with divisions and geographies.
	• Engage in a chemistry meeting to download business drivers and imperatives, communications messages and marketing campaign plans, as well as PR priorities.
	• Task the agency to review the industry area, or interview key leaders, or meet with the communications and marketing teams to solicit a number of ideas for articles.
	• Review article ideas and sign off those that fit with the business requirements; commission, review and upload as required.

Building a range of story types

I will cover how to structure your stories, articles and videos later in the book, but there are some simple approaches you can take to pinpointing stories that can help in your sourcing process.

The internal interview-led story

As mentioned previously, as any good journalist knows, stories come from people – so an obvious way to find stories is to talk to as many people as you can within your organization in different areas to uncover their stories, insights or resources that you can pull on to develop your brand journalism. Work through each business area to engage team members and investigate potential stories; arrange group meetings to surface insights, and mine out archive reports, blogs and interviews for ideas and inspiration.

NEWSROOM TIP
Building a network

A great journalist has an extensive and varied contacts list and is always talking to people to find out what is exciting and challenging them. Encourage your own team members – or challenge yourself – to think like a journalist and create your own network of story-mining contacts inside your organization.

The from-the-workplace story

If you have project work taking place in the field or on location, this is where a number of potential stories could – and should – come from. Whether you're drilling for gas, setting up clean water projects, or installing renewable energy production facilities or building a technology infrastructure, you need to go looking for story material here. You can do this remotely, with phone calls to team members, but the ideal is a trip to meet those involved and capture powerful images of what is taking place. If you can organize a foray for a brand journalism production team (potentially a writer with a smart-phone camera kit, or a camera operator or photographer) into your project or production sites, they will come back armed with high-quality stories and ideas that can keep your content flowing for some time. This might be a substantial investment but will continue to add value for many months or give content that can support your wider marketing or communications campaign.

The event-driven story

If you have a key event, gear your content towards it, including writing pre-event publicity to success stories from previous years. Drive registrations, then on the day(s) ramp up the volume of content by deploying your own news desk. Create videos, live blogs, live streaming opportunities and more to feed your social accounts and push the level of engagement out beyond just the physical attendees. Largescale internal events and conferences, as well as partner events, can be a rich source of ongoing annual material as multiple stakeholders are on one site during a short period of time.

The research-led story

Data and evidence can be a great source of story material – especially if you have a team analysing the sector, or an analyst watching competitors or trends. Working them up into potential stories and seeing where they fit with your business needs is the next logical step.

The expert-led story

If you have a team of highly experienced operators, senior managers or technical staff, you can work closely with them to deliver consistent stories. Often those who are involved in the minutiae of the everyday overlook some of the best stories around as they seem mundane or unexciting to them. Sometimes the key is to start a conversation that enables them to recognize how different or innovative or interesting a piece of work that they do is. From here, you can pinpoint interviewees through your organizational network. You can also ask managers, local managers and regional representatives to suggest individuals who may be interesting to talk to.

QUESTIONS TO UNCOVER STORIES INCLUDE:

- What are you working on that's new, different or challenging?
- What are your clients, networks and contacts being challenged by at the moment?
- What's surprised you in your work or environment over recent months?
- What innovative solutions to problems have you and your team been working on?

The online- and desk-researched story

Good journalists are always plugged into the world around them. They know what's going on and who's doing what in their 'beat' or areas of interest. They build a network and engage with contacts to find stories. While you might not be in such a position to do this, you can benefit from many of the discussions taking place online about specific industries. Websites such as question and answer site Quora can give you a sense of what some experts are discussing, as can trawling Reddit for the latest comments and news. Twitter is a great source of news and updates. Tools such as BuzzSumo and SEMrush can also tell you instantly what stories are popular and trending. Know this and you can identify ways to build on what's already been written; you can know what stories will gain traction, and you can focus attention to build a niche.

Sense-checking with an editorial board

It's entirely likely there's a wealth of great stories ready and waiting to be surfaced in your company, but they remain hidden because they sit in remote divisions or departments within the business or because these sub-units are traditionally not used to engaging with PR, communications and marketing teams.

The challenge is to first recognize that these stories are likely to exist, and then that they need to be surfaced. If you don't have one person, such as an Editor in Chief, to support a push for content, or if your team is disparate and geographically dispersed, then there is a very good case for establishing what's known as an *Editorial Board*.

Comprising area experts with their fingers more closely on the pulse, magazines often have them to ensure they're covering what audiences expect, or might be new to them. A storytelling board could well comprise divisional communications heads, as well as representatives from different geographies, or those from various different silos or networks.

Having a board allows you to pull in people who will have the guidance and insight on story development and story sourcing that you need. It doesn't have to meet all the time, or feature everyone on it every time. It can meet weekly, monthly or quarterly to drive and surface great stories. The key is that the board can help define the archetype of the 'perfect' story for your organization, while you can support the hub-and-spoke model of story mining by taking templates and story guides and pushing them down to those staff who are working directly with customers, clients or audiences.

An editorial board also can act as a dispersed or fragmented 'newsroom'. It's possible to run editorial board meetings in the same way journalists run their daily or weekly editorial meetings in order to surface great stories.

Know your rivals

Whatever the model you use to develop your story structure, rhythm and narrative, you must also understand what your competitors are saying or publishing as part of their content marketing mix. Your approach to understanding your rivals could examine the following areas.

Understand the conversations your competitors are having

To stand out within the broader narrative and across the entire industry, ideally you need to find a different line or perspective on your content – a 'clear white space' for your stories. It might be that you find a novel format or unique approach (a distinct podcast series, for instance), or find a specific take on a developing area that will set you apart. For instance, technology firms are jostling for a point of difference in the area of 5G.

Create your own qualitative analysis

Map and assess a range of aspects of competitor content in order to build a comprehensive gap analysis and comparison table. First, review their storytelling on the blog pages, or any content 'hub' spaces of their websites. Follow this up with a review of all their various platform content – including LinkedIn, Facebook and Twitter – as well as other visual and video channels if they are present on those.

Develop a competitor audit

Target a handful of your key competitors (your core competitors at this stage) and create a breakdown of what they are publishing and which digital channels they are using. Use social listening and analysis tools to understand what conversations are being had across social media by your competitors. You can use tools such as Onalytica, Pulsar or Meltwater to understand the focus of successful content and conversations.

Take the time to develop a qualitative assessment of the following aspects of your competitors' activity. This audit can also be used as the template for an analysis of your own existing content if you feel that this is required.

TABLE 5.2 The content audit process

Content audit	
For internal use, or for competitor assessment	
Volumes	The number of posts, pieces of content and social posts in total across recent weeks, months.
Cadence	An overview of the publishing rhythm and regularity of content being uploaded.
Depth and detail	An understanding of the level of detail and analysis or research that has been undertaken to create the content.
Quality	The quality of the content in terms of delivery of meaningful information, as well as the usual spelling, grammar etc.
Content themes	
Stories	An analysis of the range of the stories they are telling; this could be based on geography, range, or case study. Also, the format or approach to storytelling is useful to know.
Value to audience	The level of value and information being delivered – create overview of what type of insight it is delivering.
Themes	An overview of the themes or topics that are being covered and which of these takes priority; plus a description of any particular angle they are taking on these topics.
Theme or subject priority	If you are looking at segmenting your content into specific genres or subject areas, then log the number of articles across those specific subjects within the site – where can you find a point of difference?
Thought leadership	Analyse who stands out and why; who are the key names, speakers or spokespeople and make a note of the topics they are uncovering or discussing.
Style and format	
Tone	This analysis will allow you to see if the tone is warm and engaging or more formal; authenticity and human references also make a difference in terms of the emotional engagement content will deliver.
Writers	Do they name their writers and give them bylines? Are they 'staff writers' or do you think they have outsourced content to an agency? Are they building a personality around their key people and evangelists? Are they using influencers to write or to share content?
Length and style	Review the word length of blogs, articles and posts. Is the written content styled as listicles, or as short-form blogs with video or strong on imagery? What are they creating to catch the attention of the reader and audience?

(continued)

TABLE 5.2 (Continued)

Readability	Map and list the look and feel of the blogs or articles that have been created – for instance, are they simple text, or text with sub-headings and pull quotes, or lists? This will give you a sense of the ease of readability of the content.
Formats	Analyse the types of content that each company has created. These will include videos, graphics, infographics, listicles and buzz blogs (short-form blogs with charts and/or images and limited text).
Imagery	How are they using stock imagery, graphics and original illustrations? Is stock imagery dull and dry or stylish and engaging? This will impact shareability across social media.
Distribution	
Success	Are they getting traction with their content? If yes, what kind of results can you see in terms of shares, comments and engagement? Note the key metrics such as followers and fans on social channels, as well as shares on web or hub content.
Amplification	How is the content being shared across social media? Which sites are they using and how? What's the regularity of content uploaded, and what does it look like? What kind of traction is being achieved?
Calls to action	What are the ads, calls to action and supporting links that surround the content? If there is no brand mention, how are they building engagement or amplification for the brand?

By analysing what the competition is doing, and on what platforms and in what styles, you'll soon get a sense of where the opportunities are for a 'new' or 'different' voice. Not only will this analysis ensure your own content has a point of difference and plays a different role for the end user or audience, but it gives you an opportunity to map themes and discussions to better understand the story ecosystem. By understanding your editorial ecosystem you'll find areas that are not being tackled that you can own and inhabit. Next comes the challenge of deciding on which formats will work best for both you and your resources and team and, more importantly, for your audiences.

Notes

1 Fetterolf, J, Poushter, J and Tamir, C (2019) A changing world: global views on diversity, gender equality, family life and the importance of religion, *Pew Research Center*, 22 April. Available from https://www.pewglobal.org/2019/04/22/a-changing-world-global-views-on-diversity-gender-equality-family-life-and-the-importance-of-religion/ (archived at https://perma.cc/TR7G-3MFU)

2 World Economic Forum (nd). Available from: http://weforum.org/agenda (archived at https://perma.cc/7MJD-CDFA)

3 Papandrea, D (2016) An Inside Look at Intel iQ's Global Content Marketing Strategy, NewsCred Insights, 14 December. Available from https://insights.newscred.com/intel-iq-global-content-marketing-strategy/ (archived at https://perma.cc/5JGM-38ZL)

06

Choosing your format: audience needs and the power of text

Planning your approach

Engaging journalism, whether daily or feature-based, comes in multiple online and offline formats and from a range of different publishers and platforms. From video packages and soundbites, to live stories and audio storytelling, as well as good old-fashioned text, there is a dizzying range of ways to capture people's attention. Brand journalists too should take inspiration from, and advantage of, this increasing and accessible range of approaches to telling corporate stories.

There is a fast-increasing spectrum of available techniques and approaches to content creation – and many of them are getting cheaper and easier to deliver.

From video packages, soundbites, GIFs, animated graphics and so-called flat graphics to live stories and live coverage on social channels – there is no reason not to expand your content approaches. New means of storytelling are revolutionizing both journalism and B2B brand journalism alike; given that the typical B2B buyer will consume, read or digest at least three pieces of content before talking to a sales representative[1] (some reports even say it's more), then you will need to consider a variety of formats, depending on what outcomes you have in mind.

TEST AND LEARN

Always test what works with audiences – success and engagement might change from one day, week or one quarter to the next. If one particular format works best or is more popular then use it more and continue to measure responses. Reduce the volumes of the content that does not work. Text might be the foundation for the bulk of your stories and brand journalism initially, but experiment with low-risk approaches to other formats and analyse and respond to the results.

Research audience preferences

While there's no 'perfect' format for a piece of content, there is the 'right' format for the nature and drivers of your audience. And the key to enable you to prioritize which channels are likely to bring most success is solid research around your core audiences – where are

FIGURE 6.1 Formats for use in B2B brand journalism: text

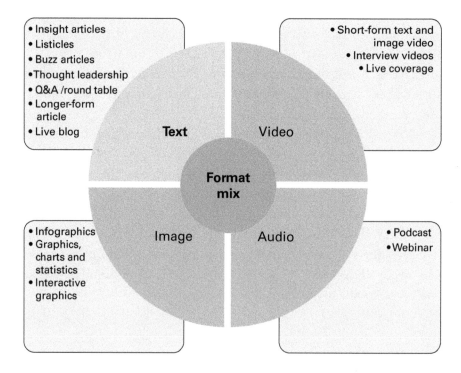

they digesting content? How long do they engage for? Do they share a particular type of format?

For younger demographics within the B2B buying journey (those who have grown up as digital natives), social media will often represent a publication or broadcast channel, rather than just an amplification channel. As research from Hubspot recently revealed: 'Younger consumers consistently show the greatest preference for social, and they treat it as a valid research channel.' As such, it adds: 'The age of your customer should play a major role in how you shape your content strategy.' It also finds that millennials engage more with video and image-based content, whilst older audiences still relate to content delivered via email. [2]

As you undertake your research, also analyse who the people are that your audiences are inspired or influenced by. According to the Demand Gen Report 2019,[3] some 95 per cent of those surveyed prefer credible content from industry influencers. Use a tool such as BuzzSumo or Sprout Social to augment your research and refine your understanding of people's preferences in terms of publishing format. Those preferences are likely to change over time as habits change and new platforms emerge. As I write this book we are seeing a resurgence in podcasting, a continuing commitment to blogs and copy, while webinars for mid-funnel communications and visual content are still popular.

Assess content according to position in the sales journey

One of the most important considerations to remember when matching format to channel is being aware of where audiences might be in their sales journey.

The brand journalism stories I have outlined in this book are created in the first instance to build brand awareness and grow a loyal audience to your publication or output. With this in mind, at the top of the sales funnel and before we even enter the sales funnel, we need to remember that we are trying to attract attention to our content and gain interest in the stories our brand is telling.

At these early stages of consideration, almost three-quarters of B2B buyers like to read blog posts and articles, with videos, e-books and podcasts also popular (according to the Content Marketing Institute[4]). In the middle stages of the funnel, white papers are most popular and – perhaps unsurprisingly – in the late stages, in the evaluation and purchase stage, it's case studies that take centre stage in terms of content needs.

The value of researching audience needs cannot be underestimated. For instance, in its content preferences survey report, 93 per cent of those interviewed by Demand Gen[5] said they wanted shorter formats in the first instance because they are increasingly time-poor and want to digest multiple pieces of content before approaching vendors or making buying decisions. The same survey also noted that content needs to be shared in a way that is 'easily digestible'. Content shared by colleagues and peers is, according to this research, the most trusted.

MATCH FORMATS TO DEVICES USED

- Research from the United States suggests more people consume content on their smartphone than on laptop devices, but the *time spent* on laptop devices content is longer than with content consumed on mobile. In addition, it finds the number of pages viewed per site visit is substantially higher on desktops than on mobile.[6]

- Research now confirms what we might have already guessed – that younger audiences use their mobiles more, whilst older demographics mainly consume content on their laptop.[7]

- Data finds time spent on websites accessed through desktop computers is substantially higher than time spent on sites from mobile devices.[8]

- While mobile devices are more popular, B2B conversion rates and engagement rates are higher from desktops than mobiles.

How to start writing great content

Research having been done, the content creation can begin and, for many brand journalists, your content will be (initially at least) about putting together enthralling copy. Since newspapers were first invented in the 1600s, the written word has been a consistently powerful medium that delivers complex and simple messages to audiences across multiple platforms.

With video and image-based media growing in popularity every year, especially with younger audiences, that is changing rapidly, and you should develop parallel content that fulfils the increasing drive of image and video for attracting audiences online. I will cover the development of image-based media and audio in the next chapter, but let's first turn our attention to text. For the moment at least, words still have impact.

Know your text 'types'

Not all text is equal, and some variations of presentation work better than others at different stages of the buyer journey, and on different platforms. Below is a guide to the types of some of the text-based content you can use. All of the types listed below build on some of the best-known approaches to story structure and/or story development that any junior reporter might learn in the first stages of his or her career. Any of them can easily comprise the bedrock of your awareness and interest-building content but some are more complicated to organize, expensive to deliver or more challenging to develop than others.

Choosing the right approach

Insight articles

If you choose to 'keep it simple' with a third-party insight article, written with a byline either by an internal team member, by an outsourced agency team or by a freelance writer, choose a story structure that works well for the type of information you are delivering. The way your articles are structured has a massive bearing on your content's readability and ability to create audience trust. There are several techniques you can use, however, to ensure your stories have resonance and impact with your readers. Scripts for accompanying videos can be lifted or re-versioned from any of these types of text article.

TABLE 6.1 Text format overview

Name	Detail	Impact vs. effort	Benefits
Insight articles	These are standard-length written articles often 600–800 words in length with two or three sub-headers They can stretch to over 1,000 words	Simple, cost-effective and low barriers to entry Focus on quality rather than just volume	Build brand awareness at the top of the funnel and continue to nurture an audience further down
Listicles	Another narrative approach for a long or short-form article, this is a considered list of grouped content or insight	The single focus listicle is a useful tool if you are looking to pique interest with a round-up The 'listicle' technique – a short article based on a list – is simple to execute	Build brand awareness at the top of the funnel and continue to nurture an audience further down
Buzz articles	These are short, sharp single-focus articles, based on a piece of research, report, chart or statistic that is then fleshed out with additional desk research	Buzz articles feed the need for short, sharp information delivered in a mixture of text and imagery Buzz pieces can cover a lot of ground in a short space of time	Buzz pieces grab your audience's attention and help build brand awareness
Thought leadership *For more information see Chapter 10 on Thought Leadership*	First-person experience-based narrative or viewpoint	Thought leadership can have high impact but the challenge is persuading senior leaders to set aside time to develop the content Thought leaders might not have natural writing or narrative creating abilities and may need external support	First-person storytelling can build affinity with your audience, and also reassures and informs
Q&A	A simple and time-effective way to create content from a one- or two-person interview. Answers can often be extended to create reports or white papers	The Q&A is a straightforward approach which is time-efficient Quality of insight will depend on the quality of the interviewee and the preparation that has been put into staging the event	Build affinity with your audience, reassure and inform

Round table report/Q&A	Often these sit in the format of Q&A but they can also be developed into a full report	An extended Q&A bringing in additional speakers is sometimes called a round table and delivers the benefit of a selection of views or opinions on a particular topic The round table can allow your brand to position itself as a thought leader or an organization with a view on an issue, by leveraging the viewpoints of others As well as brand journalism pieces, ideally you would produce a long-form piece of content from this that can be used further down the funnel	Build awareness with your audience, reassure and inform
Long-form articles	These are deep and well-researched, building on value for the audience. Their focus is on giving or aggregating information to a target audience	Time and energy should be invested to get this format right Longer pieces will deliver substantial benefits in terms of dwell time, SEO results and reputation building	Continue to build an enduring trust relationship with your audiences

Mid- and bottom-of-funnel content

White papers, research-driven articles and e-books	These formats offer research-based insight (original or desk-research), structured as a longer narrative White papers and e-books will include sub-sections or chapters to divide narrative and theme	More effort and investment is required to produce these mid-funnel content products Paid, targeted engagement campaigns (and ABM) can be built around these outputs Insight and deep dive research are of value to a technical or niche audience group in B2B	Move your audience further into the sales funnel – most often this is more technical, product-led content

The inverted pyramid approach

The simplest story construction approach is to follow the inverted pyramid – putting all the facts in descending level of importance so that all the crucial why, who, what, where and when questions are answered first.

This is the technique many journalists learn in their first few weeks on the job, and it is particularly suited to a simple narrative. It wins on its immediacy and 'scannability'. Many readers want information quickly and in bite-sized or snackable 'chunks', so you need to ensure they are pulled into the stories you create. All the vital information goes up first, while additional insight or facts follow as the story progresses 'down the pyramid'. Map the challenge, problem or issue in the first few paragraphs and add the detail as you move through the story. The further down readers go, the less 'newsworthy' the content becomes.

Clever techniques to keep readers' interest might include using an analogy at the top of the story to grab people's attention, or including a human interest reference or case study to make it more easily relatable.

The hero and villain approach

Another narrative approach that works particularly well for B2B stories is the classic hero and villain framework – the good against evil that makes stories eminently more readable.

Typically, a hero-villain story introduces the plight of characters that readers want to invest time and emotion in. They generally involve a 'hero' character, who embarks on a metaphorical 'journey' and is challenged by a crisis. The hero responds to that crisis, over-comes the challenge, and is changed as a result. This type of story structure creates empathy and a desire to read on and know what happens next. Often the story features unexpected juxtapositions or additional challenges layered onto the journey.[9]

Neuroeconomist Paul Zak's research indicates our brains produce the stress hormone cortisol during tense moments in a story, which allows us to focus, while anything with a 'cute' factor releases oxytocin, the feel-good chemical that promotes connection and empathy. Other neurological research tells us that a happy ending to a story triggers the limbic system, our brain's reward centre, to release dopamine, which makes us feel more hopeful and optimistic. Zak's research demonstrates that character-driven stories with emotional content result in a better understanding of the key points that a person (or brand) wants to get across, and that people are inherently more interested in the transcendent purpose of a product (how it will improve lives) rather than its transactional purpose (how it sells goods and services).[10]

The lesson, therefore, is to use real-life examples where you can to demonstrate how your brand has resolved the challenges presented to clients or the world at large with knowledge or expertise.

CASE STUDY

Saving the endangered one-horned rhino, one drone at a time, TCS[11]

Tata Consultancy Services' *#DigitalEmpowers* website hosts a good example of the hero and villain storytelling technique. The article tells how drones are being used by wardens in India's Kaziranga National Park in their ongoing cat-and-mouse game to tackle poaching of endangered rhinos. There is only one reference to the work of Tata Consultancy Services in the whole piece, but the message of the story is clear – technology is now saving the lives of animals and researchers. A shortened text and stock image video version of the article sits on the page and was shared on social media platforms after publication.

The resolution/drama approach

This is similar to the hero/villain approach, but is more about a protagonist (potentially supported by a brand) facing a particular challenge. Typically, the way this is structured is that the protagonist comes up with a solution that is practical, and deals with an issue of some level of adversity to a level of completion where it is resolved.

CASE STUDY

The power plant next door: Centrica[12]

This story is hosted on the content hub section (named Stories) of Centrica.com's main website. Instead of jumping in with a straightforward outline of the facts, the piece is 'humanized' and brought to life with reference to one of the homeowners taking part in the scheme:

> Suzanne Schutte is a supermarket worker – and an energy pioneer. The mother of two from Wadebridge, Cornwall is the first householder to have solar panels and cutting-edge battery technology installed as part of a £19 million trial that aims to help unlock further renewable energy use across her part of Southwest England.

It's a simple way to bring the story to life, before delving into the corporate detail.

CASE STUDY

The African country pioneering digital fishing: TCS[13]

This story, also on the #DigitalEmpowers site, frames the challenge of women fishing for their livelihoods in Senegal. The opening of the story emphasizes the challenge and introduces the resolution, before moving on to give more information and context:

> Not far from the stunning white beaches and azure waters that fringe the Senegalese town of Mbour, Anta Diouf and a thousand other women like her work in the baking heat to gut and dry fish for sale at market. It's dirty work and the hours are long, but all the effort is paying off. [...] The key to Anta's increased income? Her smartphone.

The 'What if?' approach

Much as its name suggests, this is a very simple but effective technique. The future-gazing story will pose a challenge and posit a response from a brand. Ideally you would add a human element to demonstrate the practical application of your work or insight. This helps the audience empathize and draws in the reader.

CASE STUDY

How close are we to flying in air taxis? Honeywell[14]

On the website of international US conglomerate Honeywell you will find the story of the future of Urban Air Mobility. Framed also as a 'personal story' of one man's commute in rush hour in Georgia, United States, it paints a picture of the future and the steps that will need to take place to take us there in terms of technology, infrastructure and regulation. It's a simple, effective and powerful way to take a small amount of information, research or insight and build it into a story.

I would also include 'debunking a theory or commonly held view' in this particular group. An example of this type of story might include 'Why home DNA kits might not be as private as you think'[15] (World Economic Forum).

CASE STUDY
How robots will change the world: MHI[16]

This piece is published on the MHI *Spectra* website and takes as its starting point the current disquiet around future robot development. A strong premise on which to build content for technology, innovation and industrial clients, the utopia/dystopia argument is a powerful one and enables brands to talk about how their own technology can bring a positive influence to bear in future scenarios.

The 'How to?' approach

Taking a common challenge as a jumping-off point for story development is another straightforward storytelling technique that is simple for those starting out on writing. Often you can take a single interview, or range of interviews, to create this content, and build on one single topic area. If you choose an evergreen topic with broad interest for your audience you will ensure that these articles deliver ongoing benefits as they are repeatedly surfaced from your archive, or shared in a regular ongoing pattern on your social media platforms.

The listicle

A listicle is a text or video format that delivers a list of aggregated data, facts or advice. These 'expanded lists' are a great source of credible and legitimate information and are wonderfully simple for readers or viewers to follow or navigate. They are straightforward to deliver because there is limited need for any complex narrative. Any sign-posting is also very simple.

CASE STUDY

Nine things that will kill your career: WEF[17]

Posted on the World Economic Forum's *Agenda* site, this article is written by author and academic Dr Travis Bradberry. Supported by relevant and up-to-date statistics to contextualize the premise, the piece outlines the activities that might hold you back in your career, in a simple list order. These types of lists are appealing to audiences (there's a big appetite for career and leadership content online at present) and relatively straightforward to create.

CASE STUDY

These three forces are shaping the future of global energy: MHI[18]

This piece appears on Mitsubishi Heavy Industries' *Spectra* magazine hub. It is technical, but accessible in written style, and taps into a wide and growing interest in the challenges of future energy. The structure is a simple list, but the content is insightful and intelligently written.

Whilst they are comparatively easy to build (often from various different sources gathered by a writer or researcher), attention to detail is key, so ensure the quality of your research is solid. Think of listicles that have not been produced elsewhere, or a twist you can take on a conventional approach.

> The best listicles are considered, clever and new, whilst the worst are repeats of poor-quality content or contain click-bait material that is already rife across the internet.

Listicles can range from how to live life more efficiently, how to live more healthily, to how companies can benefit from the digital revolution.[19] They can be original thought (as outlined above with Travis Bradberry's article for the World Economic Forum's *Agenda* site) or they can be curated output pulling together other people's thinking, writing or innovation.

CASE STUDY
5 coolest things on earth: GE[20]

On *GE Reports*, the well-established and successful online magazine hub for GE, the listicle is a well-established weekly format. The '5 Coolest things on earth this week' format is a regular, accessible opportunity to pull together curated stories from around the web about innovation, science and technology. This curation approach saves time for audiences by delivering high-quality, relevant stories only from credible sources.

Research by Backlinko[21] suggests that list blogs, along with 'why?' and 'what?' posts get more average social shares than other formats, as do longer headlines, in fact. Many corporates and B2B organizations are already using listicles within their blog sites. UK insurance company Hiscox, for example, has published a 'How to start a photography business: 9 steps to success' list, whilst collaboration tool Slack posted on their *Slack HQ* site[22] its 'Five employee retention strategies every company should implement'.

The buzz article

Buzz articles are short, sharp (often image-based) pieces of content you might be familiar with from news sites such as *Axios*, *Politico*, or *Buzzfeed*.

There is often a limited, but focused, amount of information contained in them – sometimes just crucial facts. *Axios* (which offers a mixture of original and narrated coverage of politics, tech, business and the media), has developed an approach it calls 'Smart Brevity'. The articles that readers first see on the site stretch to a maximum of 300 words. *Axios* then offers a shorter summary (or top line with an image underneath), with the ability to 'go deeper' with one click to access more information.

Axios's approach was developed in response to changing audience habits it noticed before launch,[23] namely that audiences *bounce* quickly, with two-thirds typically leaving a publisher's website before reading anything. It also found audiences often shared without reading

(59 per cent shared content without reading it fully). This research added to existing data that found readers were increasingly moving away from reading newspapers, and spending more time on social media sites.[24]

CASE STUDY

World Economic Forum/chart of the day: these are the world's most innovative economies[25]

Here's an example of how you can take a set of statistics or a selection of relevant charts to build a story. The short piece takes as its starting point a Global Innovation Index report produced by a group of organizations and universities. The headline teases the answer and encourages the reader to dip into the piece – lists of countries and rankings often perform well on the World Economic Forum's social media channels.

Buzz articles are a great length and type of content for B2B brand journalism. If done well these stories travel well across social media (using your chart or well-written headline as your pull), and they are quick and easy for audiences to engage with. They can give readers swift insights that – we hope – move them through the site and further into the sales funnel/journey.

The Q&A

A question and answer format can deliver swift and meaningful content results – especially if the questions are carefully planned and well thought through. If your interviewee or subject matter expert is informed and clear, the format lends itself to much faster delivery times than standard articles. The Q&A involves either interviewing a guest live (or via phone or video link) and transcribing the content, or having your guest write down answers to questions sent via email or otherwise delivered.

It's worth remembering, however, that the success or otherwise of Q&A content will be based on the *authority* of your interviewee, coupled with the *relevance* of his or her insight. You can interview someone outside of your organization (a partner, supplier or ally), or you can choose to interview someone from inside your organization (C-suite member, internal evangelist or thought leader), but you must contextualize your interviewee in the introduction.

Q&A treatment pieces also need to serve a purpose – ie has the interviewee delivered something new? Have they developed fresh insight? Have they launched a product, created a team or uncovered a new approach? Perhaps they have achieved a personal milestone, or have demonstrated specific purpose, vision or values in their work?

Before you organize a Q&A, ensure you are clear on the notional title of your article or finished piece. Consider who this is for and the purpose and value of the content. This will also help shape your questioning narrative.

Here are some other journalistic principles to guide your Q&As:

- **Do your preparation:** ensure you are briefed on the person you are interviewing. Mine for background information from internal sources.

- **Help your guest(s) prepare:** send questions through beforehand, or talk through the thrust of your story with your interviewee before you meet. This will ensure they are properly prepared and bring relevant or interesting case studies, information, statistics or evidence.

- **Use open questions:** in order to elicit broader information and stories, use *why?*, *what?* and *how?* questions. If the focus of your story is narrow, then focus them on a specific topic: 'Tell me about this...' or 'How did you approach that...?'.

- **Ask for examples:** where possible, ensure the guest substantiates their points with real-life examples of where or when they have applied a principle, or used a product or approach.

- **Flesh out where appropriate:** remember that your end game is to deliver value for your own audience or end user. Ask for more information or insight to add to what is already available in the public domain.

- **Listen:** if your interviewee drops in some information you're not familiar with, or if it sounds new or interesting, then build on that and dig deeper.

The round table

A round table is akin to a multi-person Q&A. It is an opportunity to get a range of different voices and insights on a topic in a relatively time-efficient manner. As one might expect though, organizing this type of get-together will always be a challenge. If you are trying to pull together subject matter experts from different organizations (potentially your partners, suppliers or network), this only adds to the complexity.

A 'virtual round table' could solve some of these logistical problems, with guests taking part via video or audio links. A further challenge with a round table is ensuring the discussion is moderated and driven in the direction that you need to deliver information that is new, different and coherent for your storytelling content.

Round table sessions will need to be choreographed to ensure they have a narrative arc. Moderators must understand how they need to develop and guide the discussion to ensure all areas and topics are discussed and resolved as far as possible. If the round table is live you can video the event and cut the discussion into an extended video, shorter excerpts or short-form soundbites.

Longer-form articles

The struggle to grab people's attention in today's busy world is real, but there is still an appetite for longer-form content – and you should still consider it as part of your content mix. Not only does good-quality longer content stand out from the crowd, it also gets shared in high volumes.[26] UK newspaper the *Guardian*[27] and sites such as *Ernest*[28] and *Delayed Gratification*[29] are all sites and publishers offering audiences long-form stories.

Here's why you shouldn't forget why length can be good.

READERS LIKE LONG-FORM
Research by Tom Rosenstiel of the Brookings Institution[30] shows many audiences on digital actually *prefer* longer-form content and

will enjoy longer articles. Long-form articles (including lists, aggregated thoughts from other experts etc), have long been demonstrated to be more successful for bloggers in congested content areas – as long as they are new, different and well-researched.

CASE STUDY

How to compete in a world of transient advantages: Roland Berger[31]

This piece from the *Think:Act* magazine site from global consultancy firm Roland Berger focuses on the work of Rita Gunther McGrath, a global innovation expert; the article is based on the insight included in McGrath's book on the subject of innovation. It is a substantial written piece that also includes a short-form listicle (the three-step process for your own inflection point), images and graphics.

LONGER PIECES DRIVE MORE TRAFFIC

Data from the Pew Research Center indicates that, whilst shorter news is more prevalent – and thus gets higher volumes of traffic – longer-form articles are actually accessed via mobile phone at nearly the same rate. Interestingly, it finds Facebook drives more traffic to articles in general, whilst Twitter tends to bring people who spend longer with the content. Users that come from Facebook average 107 seconds with the content, compared with 133 seconds for those who come from Twitter. It also finds that across short- and long-form content, it's Facebook that drives more referrals – about 8 out of 10 first visits from social media sites come from Facebook, compared to 15 per cent from Twitter.[32] Whilst these statistics are for traditional published news journalism, they are a useful benchmark for our own B2B brand journalism and storytelling.

LONGER ARTICLES CAN DRIVE HIGHER DWELL TIME

Analysis of Parse.ly data by Pew's researchers found consumers spend more time on average with long-form news articles than with short-form articles [short-form in this instance refers to articles that are fewer than 1,000 words]. The total engaged time for readers of articles more than 1,000 words averages about twice that of the engaged time with short-form stories – an average of 123 seconds, compared to 57.[33] Research also finds people spend more time with longer stories, that is, they are more willing to deep dive into more information if it is there. With shorter stories they skim and go.

CASE STUDY
Centrica.com/Stories[34]

Many of the articles on the Stories section of Centrica.com run to several thousand words. They are broken up with bullet points, pull quotes and multi-format content such as scrolling graphics, as well as embedded video. These longer pieces encourage a longer dwell time through engagement with the video, as well as insight from the heavily researched articles.

EXTENDED ARTICLES DRIVE SEO SUCCESS

Not only can long-form articles support your dwell time aspirations, but several studies[35] show that they will also drive traffic and generate more leads on average than shorter content. Perhaps because of this, the Content Marketing Institute's 2019 analysis of US content marketers finds 74 per cent of B2B content marketers say they've used or developed long-form content in the last 12 months.[36] Although long-form content shouldn't be created for the sake of it (it still needs to be good content), the data seems to support the fact that longer can sometimes be better.

LONGER ARTICLES ALLOW YOU TO DEMONSTRATE KNOWLEDGE

Longer-form pieces can allow you to dive deeper into a specific topic, to add maximum value to your audience. By the very nature of the space available to you, you can include more information, context or research and more keywords to boost SEO success, as well as more quotes, soundbites and information from your key people. Longer-form content can demonstrate your knowledge or expertise in a specific area, and can form the basis for an e-book that can be used further down the marketing funnel, as your audiences demonstrate an interest in a specific area, product or topic.

Arresting the scroll with your content

Whatever the technique, and whatever the format, the key attribute that will make your stories successful is their resonance with the audience. Some of that will be down to how you have researched your stories and which topics you have chosen – are they relevant to the audience you are appealing to? Some of the success of your content will be down to how you have created it, and in which format. The way it is written and the structure of the narrative itself are also crucial, as we have read. But some of your content's success will be down to how it is written – the language, tone and structure of the pieces you produce.

Here is some guidance on how you can make your written content as accessible as possible, and thereby engaging and relevant to your audience:

Keep it simple: if you are writing corporate content it can be tempting to reach for the thesaurus and include technical jargon and complex language. This will almost certainly alienate your readers. The best reporters write short sentences. They also use simple everyday language. Your aim is to get the story across in a way that is easy for readers to understand. So, avoid putting obstacles in the way. Keep adjectives to a minimum and avoid flowery prose.

Opinion, attribution and accuracy: unless you are writing a first-person piece, there is no room for antagonistic opinion in your copy. The source of facts, figures and quotes should be clear to readers. Make sure the sources you quote are credible. Do not use Wikipedia as a single source. Where possible, offer solutions to issues and challenges rather than focusing on the negative or hopeless.

Use active sentences: many people struggle with the concept of the active and passive voice. 'The cat sat on the mat' is more simple, accessible and brief than 'The mat was sat on by the cat'. The first is active and direct, while the second is passive and meandering. Active sentences tell us who did what. They give clarity to your story and it normally takes fewer words to say the same thing.

Spelling and grammar: a writer's, and a brand's, reputation is grounded in good spelling and grammar. If you struggle with these there are online tools to help you. All computers have a simple spell checker. There are also more advanced online tools like Grammarly[37] or ProWritingAid[38] that check grammar, readability and other writing errors.

Don't feel the need to paraphrase: don't be afraid to quote directly. If you have based your article on interviews with employees, experts or other spokespeople do not be afraid to include their thoughts at length. Let them talk, and judiciously transcribe what they say.

Improving on-screen readability

With so much competition for your attention, brands must make readability of their text a priority, especially as so many of us are on the move when we are digesting content.

There are some simple tips that you can use to ensure your text is more readable on screen (whether on desktop or mobile) for your audience:

- **Play to your audience:** people want information quickly. Add a summary or have bullet points at the top of your article. If they want more they'll dive deeper into the story.
- **Add clearly understandable sub headers:** this makes for ease of navigation and breaks up slabs of text.
- **Keep sentences short:** chiming with the guidance on your writing style to improve readability, it also makes sense to keep both sentences and paragraphs short; keep writing tight and to the point.
- **Have clear headlines:** choose one that excites rather than mystifies – this will also help with your SEO.
- **Break up the text:** use pull-quotes, images and pull-statistics to add variety, as well as bullet lists if relevant.
- **Vary the length of your sentences to add pace:** but remember to keep sentences tight and punchy.
- **Avoid jargon:** don't use long words, jargon or over-use acronyms when you're talking to a non-technical audience. This reinforces

the writing guidance above, and will ensure your readers can spin through your copy quickly.

- **Be bold:** phrases or quotes can be highlighted in bold to stand out.

Creating content that has authenticity and emotion

> Whether written, verbal, or visual, language is how we communicate and influence. It's how we tell our stories, and the best stories – and the best marketing – resonate on a very personal and emotional level. Writers, orators and film makers innately understand this, yet marketers don't think or do enough about it (Heidi Taylor, B2B Marketing Strategy).[39]

As we learned in Chapters 4 and 5, one of the most powerful ways to make sure your content gets the attention it needs is to ensure it is authentic. In a world where we are swamped with information, this can help make sure your content stands out. Here is some more guidance on building empathy with your B2B content:

- **Stop being anonymous:** where possible, name your writers and ideally include the opinions of your senior people; if you cannot encourage your own people to be writers, then interview your top talent and reference them in your own bylined pieces.

- **Focus on real outcomes:** if you can find examples and human stories that will exemplify your work in a natural way then try to do so. See some of the examples earlier in this chapter for inspiration.

- **Reveal more detail about the company:** tell readers about real people in the company, using real-life case studies. Case studies don't have to be bottom-of-the-funnel technical pieces. Use them as examples for your product or service.

- **Encourage team members:** support those who are keen to start creating content with guidance on editorial to enable them to start publishing and demonstrate success to others.

- **Reveal honest and genuine stories:** as we outlined in the previous chapter, use workshop settings to reveal real-life stories about challenges, outcomes, wins and losses that might deliver relatable content.

- **Lose anodyne stock imagery:** it's always a challenge, but try to find less generic ways to house, showcase and deliver your content. If you have to use stock, find ways to treat it or manipulate it to add some of your brand character or personality.
- **Reference impact and outcomes:** detail matters – reference everything that you are able to demonstrate in terms of outcomes (for instance, personal stories), not just facts and figures.

STRETCHING YOUR TEXT FURTHER

You can re-purpose your text for various platforms, ensuring you maximize its value. Consider the following:

SlideShare. Break out your copy onto slides and build a design around them. Share across the network for SEO growth.

LinkedIn. If you are the author, consider re-purposing your article with more of a 'personal prism'. Adjust the writing slightly to focus on your viewpoint more strongly. This subjective approach, or more personalized writing style, might not be appropriate for your content hub, but will work for sharing on your own LinkedIn profile.

Voice. Consider recording your longer-form written articles and sharing them as podcasts or podcast series.

Read more about how to stretch your text content even further in Chapter 7 on non-text content formats, and in Chapter 9 on distribution and amplification.

Before we move onto other formats that are available now for some powerful B2B storytelling, I shall leave the final word on written formats to the Head of Global Content Team at Red Hat, Laura Hamlyn, who puts it so well in an interview with me about balancing text content with other formats:

Words matter. But only if they are relevant, original and concise. That said, people scan. They might scan first to see if you cover what they're interested in. People also need to know what you want them to do.

What's the next step? All of this requires energy and intellect. At their best, words are an escape. They capture our attention and take us somewhere else. Whether we love reading a blog post about a software patch or watching a video about the future of farming, words/text can get us where we want to go.

Notes

1 Miller, J (2018) B2B buyers have spoken: here's what they want from your content marketing, *LinkedIn*, 18 April. Available from: https://business. linkedin.com/en-uk/marketing-solutions/blog/posts/B2B-Marketing/2018/ B2B-buyers-have-spoken-heres-what-they-want-from-your-content-marketing (archived at https://perma.cc/T2PP-NL2T)

2 An, M (2017) Content trends: preferences emerge along generational fault lines, *Hubspot*, 6 November. Available from: https://blog.hubspot.com/ news-trends/content-trends-preferences?_ga=2.79538132.1320947067. 1560881037-1945944375.1538653434#video (archived at https://perma. cc/7M8D-Y8RA)

3 Demand Gen Report (2019) 2019 Content Preferences Survey Report, *Demand Gen Report*, Hasbrouck Heights, NJ. Available from: https://www. demandgenreport.com/resources/reports/2019-content-preferences-survey- report (archived at https://perma.cc/A3WH-XZEV)

4 Content Marketing Institute (2019) B2B content marketing 2019: benchmarks, budgets, and trends – North America, *Content Marketing Institute*, 10 October. Available from: https://contentmarketinginstitute.com/ wp-content/uploads/2018/10/2019_B2B_Research_Final.pdf (archived at https://perma.cc/UD9N-C78K)

5 Demand Gen Report (2019). 2019 Content Preferences Survey Report, *Demand Gen Report*, Hasbrouck Heights, NJ. Available from: https://www. demandgenreport.com/resources/reports/2019-content-preferences-survey- report (archived at https://perma.cc/A3WH-XZEV)

6 Enge, E (2019) Mobile vs desktop traffic in 2019, *Stone Temple*, 11 April. Available from: https://www.stonetemple.com/mobile-vs-desktop-usage-study/ (archived at https://perma.cc/Y49U-BK8F)

7 An, M (2017) Content trends: preferences emerge along generational fault lines, *Hubspot*, 6 November. Available from: https://blog.hubspot.com/ news-trends/content-trends-preferences?_ga=2.79538132.1320947067. 1560881037-1945944375.1538653434#video (archived at https://perma. cc/7M8D-Y8RA)

8 Enge, E (2019) Mobile vs desktop traffic in 2019, *Stone Temple*, 11 April. Available from: https://www.stonetemple.com/mobile-vs-desktop-usage-study/ (archived at https://perma.cc/Y49U-BK8F)

9 For more information, see the work of Joseph Campbell: https://www.jcf.org/works/titles/the-hero-with-a-thousand-faces/ (archived at https://perma.cc/B7YX-ZNZ8)

10 Zak, P J (2014) Why your brain loves good storytelling, *Harvard Business Review*, 28 October. Available from: https://hbr.org/2014/10/why-your-brain-loves-good-storytelling (archived at https://perma.cc/N7R8-6R2N)

11 Muggeridge, P (2017) Saving the endangered one-horned rhino, one drone at a time, *Digital Empowers*, 8 January. Available from: https://digitalempowers.com/saving-endangered-one-horned-rhino-one-drone-time/ (archived at https://perma.cc/PTB2-XWBL)

12 Centrica (nd) The power plant next door. Available from: https://www.centrica.com/platform/the-power-plant-next-door (archived at https://perma.cc/PY8P-QKJQ)

13 McKenna, J (2017). The African country pioneering digital fishing, *Digital Empowers*, 18 December. Available from: https://digitalempowers.com/african-country-pioneering-digital-fishing/ (archived at https://perma.cc/6XTC-N39Z)

14 Honeywell (2019) How close are we to flying in air taxis? *Honeywell*, 8 June. Available from: https://www.honeywell.com/en-us/newsroom/news/2019/06/how-close-are-we-to-flying-in-air-taxis (archived at https://perma.cc/E2CJ-2BYN)

15 Fox, C (2019) Why home DNA tests might not be as private as you think, *World Economic Forum*, 9 August. Available from: https://www.weforum.org/agenda/2019/08/home-dna-tests-privacy/ (archived at https://perma.cc/46QU-6Y75)

16 Willige, A (2017) How robots will change the world, *Spectra*, 28 November. Available from: https://spectra.mhi.com/how-robots-will-change-the-world (archived at https://perma.cc/4X97-TFMN)

17 Bradberry, T (2019) Nine things that will kill your career, *World Economic Forum*, 8 August. Available from: https://www.weforum.org/agenda/2019/08/9-career-killers/ (archived at https://perma.cc/AV6D-P7RF)

18 McKenna, J (2019) These three forces are shaping the future of global energy, *Spectra*, 8 July. Available from: https://spectra.mhi.com/these-three-forces-are-shaping-the-future-of-global-energy (archived at https://perma.cc/E26V-ZYAE)

19 Leibert, F (2017) 3 things every company can do to benefit from digital disruption, *World Economic Forum*, 14 December. Available from: https://www.weforum.org/agenda/2017/12/3-things-every-company-can-do-to-avoid-digital-disruption (archived at https://perma.cc/Y6HX-U79T)

20 Worley, S (2019) The 5 coolest things on earth this week, *GE Reports*, 5 July. Available from: https://www.ge.com/reports/the-5-coolest-things-on-earth-this-week-10/ (archived at https://perma.cc/6LKB-T63A)

21 Dean, B (2019) We analyzed 912 million blog posts. Here's what we learned about content marketing, *Backlinko*, 19 February. Available from: https://backlinko.com/content-study (archived at https://perma.cc/C4TF-NWM6)

22 Slack (nd) Available from: https://slackhq.com/ (archived at https://perma.cc/BV4W-YYUL)

23 Seale, S (2018) Axios reaches today's reader with 'Smart Brevity' journalism, INMA Conference Blog, 5 September. Available from: https://www.inma.org/blogs/conference/post.cfm/axios-reaches-today-s-reader-with-smart-brevity-journalism (archived at https://perma.cc/A2WA-A23G)

24 Nielsen (2019) Time flies: U.S. adults now spend nearly half a day interacting with media, *Nielsen*, 31 July. Available from: https://www.nielsen.com/us/en/insights/article/2018/time-flies-us-adults-now-spend-nearly-half-a-day-interacting-with-media/ (archived at https://perma.cc/V4YY-7FN6)

25 Hutt, R (2019) Chart of the day: these are the world's most innovative economies, *World Economic Forum*, 30 July. Available from: https://www.weforum.org/agenda/2019/07/chart-of-the-day-these-are-the-world-s-most-innovative-economies/ (archived at https://perma.cc/F5UX-R593)

26 Blackwell, J (2018) Content marketing: beginners guide for maximum success, *Buzzsumo*, 7 November. Available from: https://buzzsumo.com/blog/content-marketing-beginners-guide (archived at https://perma.cc/N7NA-KKW9)

27 Tortoise Media (nd) Available from: https://www.tortoisemedia.com/ (archived at https://perma.cc/59L5-DBJQ)

28 Ernest (nd) Available from: http://www.ernestjournal.co.uk/ (archived at https://perma.cc/J9DC-7G3H)

29 The Slow Journalism Company (nd) Available from: https://www.slow-journalism.com/ (archived at https://perma.cc/XH4N-PF3T)

30 Rosenstiel, T (2016) Solving journalism's hidden problem: terrible analytics, Brookings Center for Effective Public Management, February. Available from: https://www.brookings.edu/wp-content/uploads/2016/07/Solving-journalisms-hidden-problem.pdf (archived at https://perma.cc/F3XB-5NMN)

31 Volyes, B (2019) How to compete in a world of transient advantages, *Roland Berger*, 25 June. Available from: https://www.rolandberger.com/en/Point-of-View/How-to-compete-in-a-world-of-transient-advantages.html (archived at https://perma.cc/CW23-WB5Z)

32 Eva Matsa, K, Mitchell, A and Stocking, G (2016) Long-form reading shows signs of life in our mobile news world, *Pew Research Center, Journalism & Media*, 5 May. Available from: https://www.journalism.org/2016/05/05/long-form-reading-shows-signs-of-life-in-our-mobile-news-world/ (archived at https://perma.cc/E8Y4-JCK4)

33 Ibid

34 Centrica Platform (nd) Available from: https://www.centrica.com/platform (archived at https://perma.cc/7VML-GU7B)

35 Zalani, C (2018) Amazing results with long-form content: 5 simple tips, *Semrush*, 19 October. Available from: https://www.semrush.com/blog/amazing-results-long-form-content-5-simple-tips/ (archived at https://perma.cc/K3EX-M42U)

36 Content Marketing Institute (2019) B2B content marketing 2019: benchmarks, budgets, and trends—North America, *Content Marketing Institute*, 10 October. Available from: https://contentmarketinginstitute.com/wp-content/uploads/2018/10/2019_B2B_Research_Final.pdf (archived at https://perma.cc/UD9N-C78K)

37 Grammarly (nd) Available from: https://www.grammarly.com/ (archived at https://perma.cc/2C2U-3BZ6)

38 Pro Writing Aid (nd) Available from: https://prowritingaid.com/ (archived at https://perma.cc/J3WA-R9DG)

39 Taylor, H (2017) *B2B Marketing Strategy: Differentiate, develop and deliver lasting customer engagement*, Kogan Page Publishers, p 32

07

Choosing your format: developing visual, video and audio content

Humans have an amazing ability to remember pictures; in fact, in a seminal study, people were able to remember more than 2,000 pictures with at least 90 per cent accuracy[1] in recognition tests carried out over a number of days. This memory for pictures consistently exceeds our ability to remember words.[2] In Mary Meeker's Internet Trends report 2019, Kevin Systrom, the co-founder of Instagram, is quoted as saying: 'People have always been visual – our brains are wired for images. Writing was a hack, a detour. Pictorial languages are how we all started to communicate – we are coming full circle.[3]

Whether you believe wholeheartedly in what Kevin Systrom has to say, the statistics bear out the fact that, in today's B2B marketing world, much of the most successful messaging is based on, or leverages, visual and graphic storytelling. As mobile phones have proliferated, they have allowed everyone to become a visual storyteller, with high-quality cameras, filters and special features that can turn the most basic image into something much more impressive. Whilst not every format is right for every brand, visual imagery is increasingly being used by most content developers in some guise or other.

According to research by the Brookings Institution into the appeal of different structures of news stories (with or without images), there's powerful evidence of the influence of non-text content online. Stories presented with a photo scored almost 20 per cent higher in engagement than stories without, whilst stories with either audio or video correlated with 36 per cent more overall engagement.[4]

Image-creation and image-sharing volumes have skyrocketed in recent years – the emergence of tools such as Facebook stories, LinkedIn Live, WhatsApp and Instagram stories as content development formats (rather than just as amplification tools) are starting to edge into regular use by B2B brands. Not only do marketers now have more platforms with which to precisely target their specific audiences, they can now pull on new formats and approaches that are more accessible, more cost-effective and quicker to test and deploy than ever before.

In this chapter I will elaborate on brands using, and experimenting with, video, audio and image-based storytelling alongside, or instead of, text output.

Your decisions about where to start in terms of format will naturally be based on what it is you want to achieve with your brand

FIGURE 7.1   Formats for use in B2B brand journalism: video, visual, audio

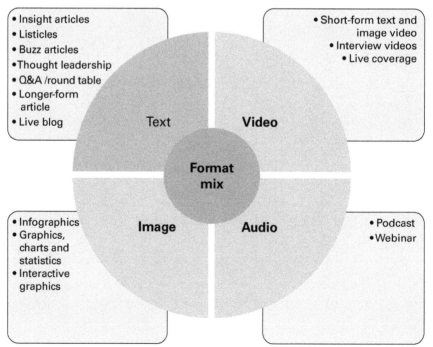

journalism, as well as the resources available to you and your own knowledge and expertise, along with the experimentation tolerance of your organization.

Video delivering brand journalism

Video content has been growing exponentially in popularity among audiences, both B2B and B2C, in recent years and, according to research, will get you more attention than your standard text content.[5] So if you have the right resources or enough budget to create it, it should be part of your content marketing mix, either as promotional/ amplification content on social media, or as a substantial part of your base content hub or cornerstone content storytelling.

It's all a question of balance. When you are deciding on your strategy, and considering your audience habits and response to content, video should be just one of the formats you consider. You will be guided by resource and budget as to what that content looks like, but ideally it will be part of your content marketing mix.

Research of a group of UK B2B marketers by LinkedIn[6] shows:

- 62 per cent of them use video for brand awareness;
- 86 per cent value video for product and service explanation;
- 78 per cent agree that video engagement helps them identify higher-quality leads;
- 57 per cent say video drives high lead volumes overall.

Millennial audiences tend to show a preference for video and as those millennials shift into buying positions in organizations, or positions of influence in the B2B buying cycle, a shift to video will be advisable.

When creating your video content, however, you need to consider the same maxims as you do when tackling your brand journalism in text format – you must develop your narrative with the audience in mind, create ideas that are of value and interest to them and consider how you will tell those stories with a narrative arc that will encourage sharing and engagement from your audience.

Video engaging audiences

Often video can be a more powerful way to engage and draw in an audience through the powerful mix of images, colour, sound and text. Consider the outcomes you are looking for before commissioning or creating your organic video and focus on:

- **Attracting attention:** we want to tell stories our audiences are interested in so they will engage in some way and thereby start to notice our brand.

- **Engaging your audience:** how can you excite with the stories you are telling? Ensure you are tapping into their needs and concerns and demonstrate very early in any piece of content why the audience should take notice of it.

- **Delivering information:** just as with our text content, you will need to offer video stories that deliver information or insight, that will help our audiences with their approach to life and/or work. Don't lose sight of the core requirements of your brand journalism, even when you are using video, graphics or images as your preferred approach.

What are the benefits of video for message delivery?

- Video can easily show and demonstrate a product, your people and your place without the need for standard words on a page.

- Moving pictures impart a large amount of information in a short time with the interlace of images, sound, music and text overlay.

- Video journalism is a way to impart passion, emotion and authenticity.

- Live coverage brings immediacy and authenticity to your messaging.

- Video enables you to build character and engagement through your real people.

- Simple new formats are emerging all the time, driven by smart phone functionality.

- Video gives the opportunity to inject character and emotion into your B2B content, with fun and engaging approaches with filters, overlays, music beds and innovative editing.

You should see video as a tool to be used all the way across your sales funnel – it can be effective to develop interest (top of funnel), to amplify (on social media platforms) as well as to dig deeper (middle of the funnel) in longer form and interviews, or Q&A formats, or to deliver more technical information (close to conversion) and to reassure after purchase.

What type of brand journalism video?

Certain video formats lend themselves to brand journalism – the type of value-add, insight-driven content you need at the top of your funnel and for driving audiences further into the consideration phase. You can either re-work or build on the same narratives and stories that you have shortlisted as part of your story-mining activity outlined in Chapter 5. Video is simply another approach to telling these stories.

Here's an overview of these video approaches in more depth.

Short-form social videos

You will no doubt be aware of the short-form videos popular across social media sites today for corporate messaging, news delivery and B2C engagement. These have many different names but they are often edited stock imagery with large, clear graphics and a music bed; generally they are short and sharp in length.

I will call these 'short-form social videos' as they are primarily used on social media platforms such as LinkedIn, Facebook, Twitter and Instagram, but they can be embedded into blog posts or used within web articles to enhance a text story. Mitsubishi Heavy Industries uses this technique on its *Spectra* website, with a short text story on electric vehicles[7] and an embedded short-form video on the page.

TABLE 7.1 Different video formats and their benefits

Format	Benefit and narrative	Channel
Short-form social video	These are incredibly popular on social media platforms where they can be viewed in their entirety, or can link through to longer-form versions or blog content. Tap into a zeitgeist issue, a key audience challenge, or deliver an explainer on an ongoing social or global problem.	Social media sites such as Facebook, LinkedIn, Instagram and YouTube
Interview video	Build intimacy and authenticity through stories from real people. This is a relatively straightforward type of production with limited need for scripting, filming days and post-production.	Website or content hub
Live video coverage	There is high engagement for live streaming on LinkedIn and don't overlook live video as a powerful tool on Facebook for business audiences.	Social media and website
Animation	Short animations from 10 to 30 seconds can stand alone as insight content or be used to promote and link through to longer-form journalism, blogs, interviews or videos. When pictures are a challenge, longer-form animations can be a useful format with which to convey information. If the subject is complicated, graphics can be a simple way to tell your story.	Social media

There is no right or wrong when it comes to length, although today many of the most successful videos are 'snackable' – short, sharp and to the point and ideally somewhere around one minute or less. The length you choose will depend on the depth and complexity of your message and the objectives of your video campaign or output; you should always test and learn as you become more experienced with video activation and creation. With the emergence of artificial intelligence-driven tools and stock footage libraries there are fewer

FIGURE 7.2 Creating short-form video

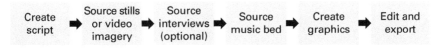

barriers to entry than ever before when it comes to creating these simple videos for use on your marketing channels or for distribution and promotion.

Step 1: Create script

Ideally you would be able to take the source narrative for your video from a pre-existing blog, article or white paper. This will give you the narrative flow to work from. Simplify the language and create one simple sentence to reflect each stage of your story. This sentence will be laid onto the video as graphics as part of the editing process.

Step 2: Stills and video

Use a stock library if you don't have access to video or stills inside your organization. Try to choose images that have people or action in them. If you have a very powerful image then use that at the start of your video to get people's attention. You will need to switch image every 3–5 seconds to keep the pace of the video up.

Step 3: Soundbites/interviews

Do not feel that you need to include interviews or soundbites, but if you have them, then they can add to the impact of your video. As the majority of your viewers will be watching with the sound down, ensure you add clear and easy-to-read subtitles.

Step 4: Music

There are multiple sources for stock music that are cost-effective and easy to access online. Match the type of music with the tone of your story – for a bold, impactful story on space travel then go for a bold track; opt for a lighter tone for your more straightforward stories. If you have access to professional editing, ideally you would edit to the beat of the music where possible.

Step 5: Graphics

Your graphics need to be created in a clear, large font that is easy to read. Ensure they stand out against your background images or video. If necessary lay dark text on a light background (or vice versa) to make them readable.

Step 6: Edit

Finally editing will mix these various assets together to create your short-form social video. You can create shorter versions for use on Instagram and Twitter, or extended versions to sit on your website or content hub. Add a call to action at the end of each video.

SOCIAL VIDEO CASE STUDY
World Economic Forum

The World Economic Forum has used short videos to great effect across its digital channels to build audiences in their millions. Videos are tightly scripted, and imagery has real punch. Videos often start with a query, challenge or unusual fact. Visit the World Economic Forum's Facebook video page[8] to see many examples of the format.

If you can, find a production device or original approach to lift your video content and make it stand out from the many videos we see today. Think back to some of the text formats for short-form articles I covered in Chapter 6, and also think of the power that video can bring for new and different outputs:

Video listicle	A numbered list or round-up is a simple way to cover a topic and to join unrelated examples.
Thought leadership	Grow your internal thought leaders and influencers with in-house short-form and extended video interviews.
Video explainer	Find an expert from your company to tackle a challenging subject or issue and outline a potential solution on video.
Q&A	The simple Q&A can be a powerful video format that is simple to produce and delivers instant insights.

INSTAGRAM VIDEO CASE STUDY

Goldman Sachs

Global investment and banking firm Goldman Sachs is innovating with video on its Instagram feed. One format is called '3 Things', digging into topics such as hybrid acceleration, healthcare sensors and consumer snacking trends. Users swipe left on the title slide to reveal three short social videos that play on a swipe and deliver more information via graphics on the topic. Goldman also uses the swipe left functionality within a format that has a still graphic with a key quote on it from a spokesperson; a swipe left reveals a short video clip of that person.

Interview video

Interview videos are straightforward to produce and can give instant value to the viewer. They are a simple way to develop thought leadership content that has instant impact, as video footage enables audiences to immediately relate to the human behind the message. Ensure you use captioning or subtitles on all video interviews as the majority of video viewed online and on social platforms is viewed with the sound down.

They are often used for longer, more thoughtful insight delivery and can take a variety of formats (many of which you will be familiar with from watching nightly news bulletins), for instance:

- Single soundbite interview: short, sharp, to the point. Edited with subtitles and generally used on social media platforms to deliver a single insight point and push audiences to engage to find out more.

- One person interviews or talks with another (a 'one plus one'): a longer format where one person interviews another. Trail these on social and host on your website or YouTube.

- If you have access to multiple cameras, or are confident in the format, and your presenter, then consider multiple interviewees (one plus two) from live events.

- Selection of soundbites: take a selection of interview clips and edit them together into a narrative or montage to outline a particular theme or experience.

Interview video is ideally filmed with one person in shot in a 'medium close-up' framing that shows their head and shoulders, or top half of the body. You can zoom in even more closely when you are finalizing your video. Video with close-ups of faces will engage your audience more than a wider shot where you can only see your speaker or the image in the distance.

NEWSROOM TIP

Frame it right

For your brand journalism interviews, film your interviewee speaking 'off camera' (that is, looking slightly to the left or right of the lens) rather than directly into the camera lens. Consider using graphic 'chapter headings' to segment answers or content sections delivered by your interviewer. If the message to be delivered is a powerful one, that has a single sense of urgency, then consider adjusting your speaker's eyeline to be 'down the barrel' (ie directly into the lens) for intimacy and impact.

Stretching your video interviews further

If you are using an external agency or professional video team to create your video it can be a sizeable commitment, both in terms of time and budget. Create a plan beforehand for how to get as much value out of your content as possible, considering alternative and additional formats that you can create from your original raw (rushes) footage.

The interview video is versatile in that you can take the original material and use it in a multitude of ways:

- Prepare your questions carefully so that you are able to strip the audio from the interview video and edit it into a podcast format.

- Develop a transcript from the video for upload to enhance SEO and give wider access to your material.

- Use the insight from video interviews to develop parallel written material, either grouping subject matter or considering a single topic.

- Edit powerful soundbites for even shorter-form social sharing teasers.

Live video coverage

If your company or organization can tolerate the stress of live broadcasting – and any potential risks associated with it – then live coverage is a really powerful tool and brand journalism approach. Just as news shows report live from events and news story locations, why shouldn't you, as a brand, take ownership of your live coverage on your own owned channels? Emerging tools such as LinkedIn Live and Facebook Live make brand broadcasting simpler than ever.

The benefits of going live with your brand journalism

- Build a relationship with distributed audiences.

- Demonstrate the value of your products and insights.

- Grow awareness of your brand with your own people as influencers, journalists and commentators.

- Build immediacy into your brand message – demonstrate your knowledge.

Today there are no end of options for the B2B marketer to deliver live coverage across the platform mix. Smartphones combined with the most rudimentary technical kit, such as an external microphone and tripod, give all brands the opportunity to go live; if budget and resources allow, you can develop a multi-camera, multi-location solution.

When to go live

Live, real-time coverage for your corporate events (small or large) is a highly effective means of getting attention for your brand and leveraging the energy of a particular event or experience. The ideal situation is to offer insight and information from an event where you have multiple guests, an engaged audience and a range of potential interviewees – this could be an internal event such as a supplier or vendor event, or it could be a sponsored event where you, the brand, have pulled together various stakeholders or partners to discuss a particular issue, challenge or business trend.

Try to have either some activity in the area or something of value to say, as the key to your live coverage is – just as you see on the nightly news – either activity or insight. There are dozens of largescale global industry events that you can no doubt consider as the backdrop for your live coverage. You will need to assess which is the best event to give you the opportunity to develop your own live news output, and how you might go about creating that output. Do not be intimidated by the task – today's smartphone technology can enable even the smallest B2B player to 'go live', albeit with a more restrained aspiration than a multinational.

CASE STUDY
Gartner on LinkedIn Live

Gartner launched its *Smarter with Gartner* series on LinkedIn Live as another platform to engage audiences with its insight and thought leadership. The most recent episode – a half-hour interview with a senior VP at the research company – gained more than 80,000 views and more than 800 comments.

Where to stream live coverage

There are many ways to easily stream video, information and interviews from your own internal events, or external events that you are visiting, exhibiting at or attending:

Website: depending on the purpose of your live video coverage you can either stream live to your own website using a service such as

YouTube with embed software, or an alternative such as Vimeo's Livestream technology. Either way the set-up is relatively straightforward for your tech team or outsourced video agency.

Social channels: more platforms are adding live or near-live functionality. Increasingly we are seeing B2B brands live on:

- **Facebook:** use Facebook Live functionality to interact with audiences. Network security company Juniper Networks uses the functionality for Q&A sessions with its experts. Also look at the World Economic Forum's Facebook page for regular live sessions from the Annual Meeting in Davos and the Forum's own Book Club.

- **LinkedIn:** apply directly for broadcast capabilities through LinkedIn Live and use the platform for live streaming of content such as interviews and corporate events.

- **Instagram:** Instagram Stories enable you to publish and track your activity and can be useful for event coverage; unlike other Instagram posts they allow you to include a link. Instagram live functionality is also available.

CASE STUDY
Cisco on LinkedIn Live

Cisco is using LinkedIn Live functionality for delivery of live interviews with staff to its 2.5 million audience to discuss the culture of the company. Topics include work/life balance and interviews with interns.

Using imagery for your complex storytelling

Images, graphics and infographics perform well, as I have already said, when added to your written content, but they are also an obvious format to be turning to with the ever-increasing popularity of social platforms that are focused on imagery and visuals. Imagery and social sharing formats should be developed, ideally, in parallel with the original piece, either to be embedded or used as part of your social media campaigns on LinkedIn, Twitter, Facebook, Instagram and other social sites.

Infographics

There is a huge range of infographics that you can use to tell complex stories within your brand journalism mix. They are an alternative to text, and can help to enhance or supplement a pure text article.

Infographics can be a substantial investment of time and money but can prove to be a great format that you can 'slice and dice' into additional social media imagery from your larger design. Infographics can help as a tool for search engine optimization in general terms as visual assets, but they can also be used further down the funnel for engaging with very specific audiences on focused topics of narrower interest. Whichever outcome you are looking for, here are some key principles to consider before embarking on an infographic build:

- **Evergreen:** choose a subject that will have a long shelf life and that you can continue to use over a period of time. There is little point investing in a large and complex infographic if it will only have a short window of use.

- **Structure:** create a draft script or storyboard for your infographic as early on in the process as possible. This might be something you commission your agency or graphics department to do, but (whoever does it) ensure you have a clear view of the 'journey' through the graphic before it is built or finalized.

- **Research:** look at what others have designed and built to decide what you want to create before you commission or issue a brief. Often infographics will be produced by an agency or outsourced graphic design team. The biggest challenge for agencies is to visualize what a client is imagining – one person's infographic may look very different to another's.

- **Invest:** invest the time and money in proper research to back up the information in your infographic. Make sure you have enough depth in the data you are intending to use. Thin data will not deliver a good outcome.

In formatting terms, remember:

- Top-to-bottom scrolling works for your infographics so ensure they are built to be read from top to bottom as audiences scan through them on desktop and mobile.
- Narrative arc: ensure there is a narrative arc in your infographic – that you are laying out your story (perhaps a challenge, with solutions and an outcome) as clearly as you would a written or video piece.
- Brand colours: where possible work with your brand palette to ensure consistency of look and feel across your channels.
- Legibility: too many infographics are not easy to read and digest. Ensure your colours and font choice and size work for maximum readability.

Graphics, charts and statistics

You and your team can create simple graphics to help supplement or tell your stories. Charts and statistics can form the basis of your short buzz articles, as I outlined in the previous chapter. A range of charts – or a deep-dive into a longer report using graphics as the primary means of telling the story – can be an option for an alternative way of getting your message across. Charts also perform extremely well on social media platforms as shareables to grow awareness of your stories.

Make sure any charts are well-referenced and come from a reputable source, if not your own research. Ensure they are clear and easy to read and deliver a clear visual message in a short amount of time. Also make sure they have a specific title that clearly outlines what is included in the image.

CASE STUDY

5G in industrial operations: Capgemini[9]

This chart-based piece clearly maps the story of 5G and its impact on industrial operations. It has been built as a lengthways list of standalone facts with charts and graphics, but also works as a full narrative, reflecting the contents of a deep-dive report that users can click through to.

Animating and interactive graphics

Animations dropped into your longer articles, or supplementing your articles and text pieces, can increase dwell time and help with sharing and engagement. Consider pulling out one theme from the longer piece, or encapsulating the entirety of the story in your animations.

Audio: the rise of podcasting

Audio content is growing in popularity as audiences seek new formats for digesting extended material. Podcasting, particularly, has grown hugely in the UK and the US, with audiences looking to the medium to extend the radio experience.[13,14]

More than a third of those polled by Edison Research said they had listened to a podcast in the last month – a figure that's been rising every year since 2013 – and the average podcast listener listens to seven a week. According to some research, more than 60 per cent of B2B buyers describe podcasts as a content format that they value in the early stages of the buying process.[15]

Numbers are growing, and those who enjoy their podcasts tend to become passionate about them, but in reality many brands do not have the commitment to this publishing medium that a 'regular publisher' will have. Podcasts, for one thing, take a surprising amount of work to develop and create – from building the strategy, finding recording locations, choosing and booking an available guest, planning the questions, recording, editing and then uploading.

Laura Hamlyn, Head of the Global Content team for software company Red Hat, explained to me how the company sources ideas and remains audience-focused with its podcast, *Command Line Heroes*.[16] One of the aims of the series is building brand awareness and affinity through the use of Red Hat and non-Red Hat voices.

> For our podcast, we started a listening tour focused on different tech events around the world. We have conducted hundreds of interviews with our target audience, asking them about their careers, how they got started (their origin story), what they're working on now, and what inspires them. We also share ideas for podcast themes with a wide variety of Red Hat employees from across our business, because many of them represent our target audience. Our team also monitors influencers to understand what they think is important, and we try to step out of the main storyline a few steps to see if there's a tangential connection point we can make.

Creating a successful podcast

You can develop a strong and loyal followership via podcasting (there's something intimate and authentic about a piece of voice content), but the challenge for most B2B and corporate marketers when it comes to this format is maintaining consistency and flow. As those of us who have ever created a radio programme can confirm, it takes time, energy and effort to make a high-quality piece of audio content – and if you are attaching your brand to that output it's important that you get it right. Here are some considerations before you get started:

Commit to a series: if you are dipping your toe in the water with podcasting then commit to a short series, rather than launching a weekly podcast and then not being able to sustain that. A series can be promoted as a short run and if you run out of steam (or do not hit your targets or KPIs) then you can always divert resources elsewhere.

Audience first: what do your audiences need or want to know and how can you help them? Just as when we were looking at developing stories for your brand journalism as a whole, you need to consider what you are talking about and why each week or each episode and ensure you are delivering value.

Clarify your outcomes: what do you want to achieve from your podcast and how will it deliver? If you are clear on who your podcast is for, and what you will talk about, then you will be more successful. For instance, Trader Joe's broadcast is for internal staff and communications and the name reflects that, as does the content. It gets great reviews from internal team members on the podcast apps from where it is available.

Get a host: if you can find someone internal who is relaxed and charismatic enough to host your podcast then that's great – you might even find two if you scour your communications and marketing departments. But if you can't find your 'talent' in-house then use a freelancer, or better still, an influencer or blogger to give you instant credibility. Red Hat marketing – which noted it has more than half a million downloads of its podcast after season 2[17] – uses ambassador and expert Saron Yitbarek to tell its story on its podcast.

Focus on quality: as with any content you produce with your brand attached to it you need to produce output of quality. Ensure you, or your presenter or producer (or your agency if you have outsourced the work), have done the homework and have prepared questions to ensure you will deliver the story that is required for the audience, pitched at the right level and with the right messaging.

Find your voices: consider who you will interview in your podcast and what they will talk about. Ensure your theme will stretch across multiple episodes and still be of interest to your audience. Ideally a brand would source many of its speakers (either the host or the guests) from its own ranks, but it also adds to authenticity and brand journalism credentials to interview others who will chime with the values of your brand, or have insights that will be of value to your audience.

PODCAST CASE STUDY
Dell Luminaries

The Dell Luminaries podcast is a standout. Titles for its programming including industry-focused episodes such as '5G is coming... to transform connectivity' and broad, news-type content such as 'Promoting diversity in the tech industry... by design'. The podcast is a great case study to emulate. Why?

- It is consistent and regular, and includes guests from Dell, from its partners and analyst network.

- It has knowledgeable and professional hosts (Mark Schaefer and Douglas Karr) who add value to the overall programming and discussion.

- The full range of formats and outputs is included – there is a transcript, plus detailed introduction and full background information.

- It is easy to access and digest – the descriptions include bullet points on what you'll learn, for instance, encouraging you to engage.

- The text accompaniment is easy to read, with variety in the text, pull quotes and a focus on quality etc.

- There is a biography of each guest outlining who they are and why you should listen.

Learn from these other B2B podcasting examples

Home Depot: Give me an H:[18] – overview of Home Depot's sustainability work and credentials, values-based culture, and what it's doing to ensure its supply chain is robust. This sits well as part of their internal communications marketing suite and has got engagement in the thousands.

Inside Trader Joe's:[19] culture and behind the scenes. Trader Joe's podcast goes behind the scenes and interviews people working there. It's humorous and light-hearted, and goes into stores to unpick aspects of the company values and culture. Internally focused, it's of value for internal staff and potential recruits.

Leadpages.net: The Lead Generation:[20] the series features conversations with entrepreneurs being honest about their work and challenges. It is consistent and the format and design of the hosting page is clear. Each podcast page includes:

- five bullet points on key takeaways from the podcast;
- a transcript of the conversation (making that content work harder for SEO);
- links and listings of all resources mentioned in the podcast;
- some suggested discussion topics for those who have listened to the podcast;
- follow-up calls to action.

Notes

1 Standing, L, Conezio, J and Haber, R N (1970) Perception and memory for pictures: single-trial learning of 2500 visual stimuli, *Psychonomic Science*, **19** (2), pp 73–74

2 Shepard, R N (1967) Recognition memory for words, sentences, and pictures, *Journal of Verbal Learning and Verbal Behavior*, **6** (1), pp 156–63

3 Bondcap (2019) Internet Trends 2019, *Bondcap*. Available from: https://www.bondcap.com/report/itr19/ (archived at https://perma.cc/C96Z-YR5E)

4   Rosenstiel, T (2016) Solving journalism's hidden problem: terrible analytics, Brookings Center for Effective Public Management, February. Available from: https://www.brookings.edu/wp-content/uploads/2016/07/Solving-journalisms-hidden-problem.pdf (archived at https://perma.cc/D94E-NDRT)

5   An, M (2018) Content trends: preferences emerge along generational fault lines, *Hubspot*, 14 December. Available from: https://blog.hubspot.com/news-trends/content-trends-preferences?_ga=2.79538132.1320947067.1560881037-1945944375.1538653434#video (archived at https://perma.cc/T5PV-JBPF)

6   Bunting, J (2018) Welcome to the era of B2B video, *LinkedIn Business*, 16 April. Available from: https://business.linkedin.com/en-uk/marketing-solutions/blog/posts/B2B-video/2018/welcome-to-the-era-of-b2b-video (archived at https://perma.cc/24CD-Z43T)

7   Mitsubishi Heavy Industries (2019) Electric cars are powering buildings from parking lots, *Spectra*, 12 June 2019. Available from: https://spectra.mhi.com/electric-cars-are-powering-buildings-from-parking-lots (archived at https://perma.cc/4FTN-AHAS)

8   World Economic Forum Facebook Videos (nd). Available from: https://www.facebook.com/WEFvideo/ (archived at https://perma.cc/ADC4-GMXE)

9   Capgemini (2019) 5G in industrial operations: how telcos and industrial companies stand to benefit. Available from: https://www.capgemini.com/wp-content/uploads/2019/06/5G_Infographic.pdf (archived at https://perma.cc/R9MK-Y7VV)

10 Bostock, B (2019) These 12 charts show how the world's population has exploded in the last 200 years. World Economic Forum, 15 July. Available from: https://www.weforum.org/agenda/2019/07/populations-around-world-changed-over-the-years/ (archived at https://perma.cc/UJW2-W4FW)

11 Centrica (nd) AI is personalizing energy for customers. Available from: https://www.centrica.com/platform/ai-personalising-energy (archived at https://perma.cc/A2TF-FLKL)

12 The One Brief (nd) Edge, fog or cloud? How the Internet Of Things is shaking up how – and where – data are handled. Available from: https://theonebrief.com/edge-fog-or-cloud-how-the-internet-of-things-is-shaking-up-how-and-where-data-is-handled/ (archived at https://perma.cc/G2S4-USPV)

13 Ofcom (2018) Podcast listening booms in the UK, *Ofcom*, 28 September. Available from: https://www.ofcom.org.uk/about-ofcom/latest/media/media-releases/2018/uk-podcast-listening-booms (archived at https://perma.cc/MSC8-ALCR)

14 Edison Research (2017) The Infinite Dial 2017, *Edison*, 9 March. Available from: https://www.edisonresearch.com/infinite-dial-2017/ (archived at https://perma.cc/WQD8-W38G)

15 Miller, J (2018) B2B buyers have spoken: here's what they want from your content marketing, *LinkedIn*, 18 April. Available from: https://business. linkedin.com/en-uk/marketing-solutions/blog/posts/B2B-Marketing/2018/ B2B-buyers-have-spoken-heres-what-they-want-from-your-content-marketing (archived at https://perma.cc/4G6B-PW9X)

16 Red Hat (nd) Red Hat Command Line Heroes. Available from: https://www. redhat.com/en/command-line-heroes (archived at https://perma.cc/3GXE-D83M)

17 McHugh, A (2019) What making a podcast taught us about branded content, *Red Hat*, 6 March. Available from: https://www.redhat.com/en/blog/what-making-podcast-taught-us-about-branded-content (archived at https://perma. cc/62FR-F7YX)

18 The Home Depot (nd) Give me an H. Available from: https://podcasts.apple. com/us/podcast/give-me-an-h/id1321640155 (archived at https://perma. cc/4SZR-6PWR)

19 Trader Joe's (nd) Inside trader Joe's. Available from: https://podcasts.apple. com/gb/podcast/inside-trader-joes/id1375630453 (archived at https://perma. cc/3CK8-ZQSR)

20 Lead Pages (nd) Podcast: The Lead Generation. Available from: https://www. leadpages.net/blog/category/podcast-the-lead-generation/ (archived at https:// perma.cc/5R3X-UJLW)

08

Content hubs: finding a home for your stories

Finding the right location to house good-quality journalistic content can be a challenge. If your organization is starting to develop regular thought leadership or story-based content then it will need a dedicated space that is potentially broader than a simple blogs page on a corporate website. Your corporate stories require a taxonomy or structured system that's easy for users to navigate. This will help pull audiences further into your site, increasing dwell time or time on site and thereby building on your brand awareness and association outcomes. Every audience member who has engaged with your content and clicked back to your site is an opportunity for conversation and potential conversion.

A dedicated space, hub or microsite is a way to ensure you can measure engagement and traffic to stories; you can also build an audience interested in one specific area, industry or topic, or who will build an affiliation with your brand or message. A dedicated content hub will allow you to amplify via newsletter distribution and social media posting, pushing audiences back to a content hub, rather than simply through to a single story hosted on social or a non-proprietary website where the potential journey through a site to sale is lost.

Many brands who are experienced in the content space have a specific tab on their web navigation bar for brand stories. As companies have moved through the content development and thought leadership maturity curve, they are now more likely to badge these pages more creatively.

So we see *Eniday* (Eni), *Insights* (from Agilitylogistics.com), *enterprise.nxt* (HPE),[1] *Knowledge Centre* (from UPS)[2], *Walmart Today*[3] or *Perspectives* (from Dell Technologies & IBM UK Think).[4] Other brands have content hubs for specific target audiences, specific divisions or areas of content – see *Txchnologist* (from GE).

Taking the blog to the next level

Rather than simply publishing to a 'blog' site on your website, your organization may choose to commit more resources, focus and budget to a standalone site that is more like a publication – it may be designed to look more like a digital magazine, or it might have an approach to publishing that warrants the development of a stan-dalone 'site within a site'.

Either way the hub can be a home to your themed content that can be badged or branded to align with your overarching brand values and to engage your target audiences. Once you've built up a regular flow of material and grown your audience, you have built a base on which to develop paid and branded engagement. Interviewed for this book, leading content strategist Robert Rose is emphatic about the need for corporate commitment to content, in whatever guise:

> The real key in my mind is that what most brands miss is they don't build a platform, they don't build a publication, they don't build a centre of gravity around content. What they do is they build just asset, after asset, after asset, that lives in a disaggregated format on their website. And so content piece number 1 doesn't work any harder for them than content piece number 473. Building that library, that magazine, that resource centre, that centre of gravity where content is going to be discovered, is truly the most important part. People don't just subscribe to individual pieces of content; they subscribe to a regular communication and insight. That's the key to creating an audience, and it's what most brands don't do. Instead they look at content as an asset that drives a transaction, which for them might be a registration or an entry into a marketing database – and they call that an audience.

That's not an audience, that's just somebody who transacted for a piece of content. A subscriber is someone who wants to get the next piece of content. That shift in perspective is the most important aspect of how to build an audience these days, versus just a transactional set of marketing entries in your database.

The standalone brand name

By appropriating the look and feel of a magazine or online publication with a standalone brand name you not only map your themes clearly for a more pleasing user experience, you also pull your user through the site and encourage more engagement with your articles, unfettered by other content that might distract on a corporate website.

Sites like *i-CIO* (Fujitsu) or *CMO* magazine (Adobe) are good examples of pure focus content hubs with clear audience value. The sites are not dominated by highly visible branding but instead deliver value in the insight and information they offer, albeit underpinned by

FIGURE 8.1 Approaches to story hub structure

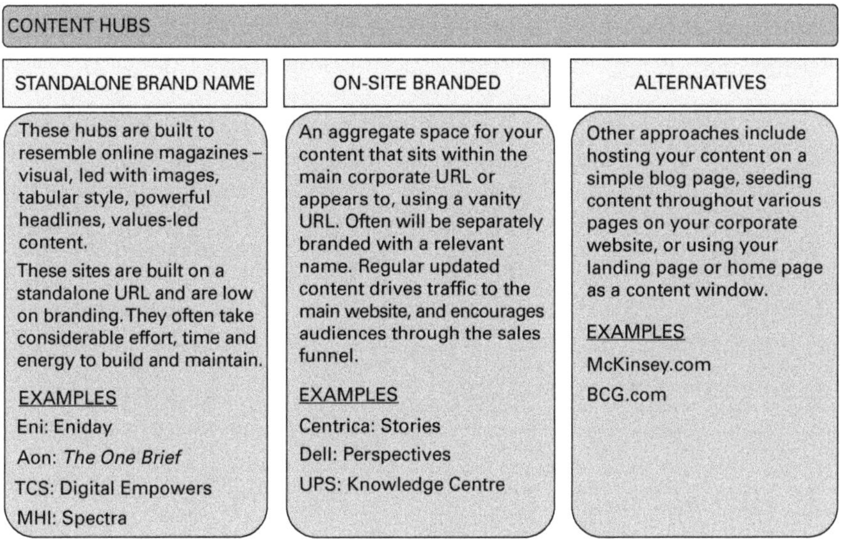

CONTENT HUBS

STANDALONE BRAND NAME	ON-SITE BRANDED	ALTERNATIVES
These hubs are built to resemble online magazines – visual, led with images, tabular style, powerful headlines, values-led content. These sites are built on a standalone URL and are low on branding. They often take considerable effort, time and energy to build and maintain. EXAMPLES Eni: Eniday Aon: *The One Brief* TCS: Digital Empowers MHI: Spectra	An aggregate space for your content that sits within the main corporate URL or appears to, using a vanity URL. Often will be separately branded with a relevant name. Regular updated content drives traffic to the main website, and encourages audiences through the sales funnel. EXAMPLES Centrica: Stories Dell: Perspectives UPS: Knowledge Centre	Other approaches include hosting your content on a simple blog page, seeding content throughout various pages on your corporate website, or using your landing page or home page as a content window. EXAMPLES McKinsey.com BCG.com

brand examples and a light touch or proprietary promotion. In the main the content and stories within these sites – and others such as the long-established *GE Reports*[5] – are informative, high quality and of standalone interest and value.

Most of these sites have a bold and impactful front page with strong imagery in a mobile responsive design. The magazine is generally branded with a distinct name and is separate to the company's main website; ideally look to subtle branding (often this is on the footer page or top right as a simple logo). If you do choose an online magazine format, remember your front page is an opportunity to mix bold imagery with some cracking headlines that not only encapsulate your story but engage your user or reader.

These content hubs are often staffed like magazines – they'll have a dedicated content team led by an editor with a clear sense of mission and purpose and a standalone budget with which to purchase or commission content. Some of the best examples of these sites have been in existence for many years and have built considerable audiences in that time, attracted often by specialist knowledge and a consistent tone of voice and quality of content. The standalone site *Eniday*[6] (described as a project by energy supplier Eni.com, with light Eni branding) tells the stories of 'new frontiers in the sector and of the people who work every day to transform the Earth's natural resources into energy'. It is focused on promoting positive stories around energy.

Aon's magazine *The One Brief*[7] bills itself as a space that brings audiences 'thought-provoking perspective from experts from around the world'. It delivers content on an expert, professional level, focusing on an audience of business leaders. Senior Manager for Content, Global Marketing, Venetta Linas Paris, says that the company designed *The One Brief* as a 'champion of brand journalism' that helps the company articulate more clearly their narrative across varying points of view to give a broad set of audiences insight on various important topics.[8] She wanted to shift the audience from a general brand awareness of Aon to a clear understanding of the breadth of topics that they cover.

CASE STUDY
GE Reports

How do you tackle communicating with broad, worldwide audiences if you are a company with a history of more than 120 years, and more than 280,000 employees around the world? This is the challenge for GE, which is known for its innovative approach to content. Long thought of as the 'poster child' of corporate storytelling, the *GE Reports* hub is at the heart of the GE content marketing play, attracting hundreds of thousands of readers every month with its *Wired*-style articles focusing on science, tech and innovation. Editor in Chief, GE, Tomas Kellner, says he wanted to ensure that the magazine tells people something new. He has spoken about focusing '100 per cent on storytelling', creating stories with 'real protagonists' and 'real outcomes'.[9] Kellner also dictates that all pieces published in *GE Reports* must tell the reader something new that they won't have known before. Kellner is the author of many of the stories on *GE Reports* and travels the world to seek them out and report on them, but the network of regionalized sites is also supported by market-level agencies and partners to deliver more targeted, localized content. Kellner writes:

> It's a news hub where thousands of readers come every day for news and opinions about the latest technological breakthroughs and developments, including the future of medicine, power generation and aviation. It's also a place where investors learn how GE makes money.[10]

On-site or standalone magazine?

The brands outlined above have committed to building an offsite brand with a clear masthead. That's a long-term commitment of resource. Many other brands have chosen to house their content hub on their main website – either independently branded (for instance, the World Economic Forum's *Agenda* site) or simply delivered as Insights or Perspectives.

These sites might not have the benefit of being a standalone brand, but nonetheless can be a suitable way to create a home for your brand journalism.

Establish clarity of vision and mission

Most of the hubs outlined in this chapter are well resourced and have been in existence for some time. They've grown, engaged audiences and proven their worth for communications and marketing teams.

As with all of your brand journalism, establishing a clear mission for your output is important from the start. If you want to commit to a regular, dedicated publication (whether niche in subject or broad in interest) you will need substantial time and resources on the project. Review the chapters on 'establishing your strategy' to understand how you can map your aims and audiences, as well as your outcomes.

Whatever the nature, size or background of your audience, they need to feel that the content that's hosted on the site is relevant, targeted and of value. Ensure you have done your groundwork before you start on what areas are of interest. The content should tap into a specific area of interest, niche or industry priority – or a story they feel is relevant to them or their business – and it needs to offer a solution or insight. Carry out a competitor audit (discover how to in Chapter 5 on story mining) before you start to map exactly where there is a place for your focus or subject area.

UK-based energy and services company Centrica developed its content hub – called Stories, and hosted on the main Centrica website – with specific targeted audiences in mind, and a longer-term approach to winning, as former Director of Digital Communications Laura Price explained:

> When we created our content hub, we never intended for it to be a quick win; it was never going to be something where we did a couple of stories and then we'd go back to our old methods of communication. We took it really seriously, and it was going to become the mainstay of our communications activity. The brilliance of this was that often, in an organization, you are waiting for news to be delivered to you internally by business units that you can then publish, or you are waiting for something to happen. When you are commissioning and creating your own content for your own content hub, you are in total control of what you're putting out and when you're putting it out – it was always a long-term play for us.

Global IT multinational Tata Consultancy Services created its standalone content hub, *Digital Empowers*, as the heart of a single campaign, launching it at the World Economic Forum in Davos. The theme is the need to demonstrate where tech can 'do good', according to TCS Chief Marketing and Communications Officer (Global Markets) Abhinav Kumar:

> We launched the Digital Empowers campaign and site to promote a more progressive and positive view of the potential of digital technologies. Too much of the current narrative on technology in the media today is negative (job losses through automation, privacy encroachment, cybersecurity breaches etc) and we wanted to also bring out the other side of the coin – all the good that technology has enabled for humans. The platform was focused on bringing out the stories from us and our partners on where technology is being used to do good. We built a mobile app for farmers and fishermen that gives them access to information they might not have had in the past, for instance, empowering them with pricing, market and weather information. Armed with a better understanding of prices, they are able to secure better value for their produce and reduce their dependence on intermediaries who have historically preyed on them. We want to bring out the positive impact of technology. Using stories to deliver messages is not a new trend – we've known about the impact of stories since we were hunter gatherers, and the emotional connection that stories can bring is not new. We want these stories to capture people's attention, and keep it.

Find the right stories

How do you find the right stories for your content hub? There is more detail in Chapter 4 on 'Finding the narrative', but here is an overview of how to get started:

1 Start with your business aims or priorities – where is the company or organization going and what are the product areas, geographies or services it is offering?

2 Map the interests of your audiences using a tool such as Onalytica, Radarly or Pulsar. There are many other tools on the market, and all will be able to segment what your target audiences are interested in and what they are discussing online.

3 Create a list that represents a minimum of a dozen challenges that your audience faces in their business lives where your viewpoint would be welcomed or can service a purpose:

   a. Think high level first:

     – How do they keep up with the changing landscape?

     – How do they ensure they have the right skills and knowledge to succeed in the future workspace?

     – How do they understand some of the key challenges of their industry? What are these challenges?

   b. Move into more specific topics that are related to their specific area of expertise or industry:

     – What are the key influences on the business landscape?

     – How are others responding to these influences and challenges?

     – What is best practice in this arena, industry or sector?

4 Once you have developed your headline narratives or areas of interest you can build your editorial team or news team to support story mining and story surfacing from within your organization. You can read more about these techniques in Chapter 5.

High-quality content for specialist audiences

Successful content hubs are those that host stories with impact, provide value for discrete audiences and signpost clearly what's on their site. A hub such as SAP's *D!gitalist*[11] offers a wide range of content aimed at the C-suite and executives in the broad technology space, but much of its content is broad, wide-ranging and of general interest to a range of audiences. By creating stories that are simply interesting and easy to read, the *D!gitalist* team has created a great hub that offers ongoing value and a real reason to subscribe. Content ranges from high-level business insight tackling issues such as diversity and the future of work, through areas of interest more closely aligned to the broad technology sector (CIO knowledge, CFO knowledge) through stories much more closely linked to SAP's business offer such as cloud and cybersecurity. Stories are segmented again on the site using two indexed menus encompassing customer experience, the digital economy, machine learning and the Internet of Things.

A site such as SAP's *D!gitalist* leverages content from across this huge organization, with contributors coming from all areas, sectors and geographies and able to deliver content that can be relevant across the wide range of topics covered by the site. Krista Ruhe was, until recently, Editor in Chief of *D!gitalist Magazine* for SAP, and explained the concept and approach of the site to me:

> I think it's essential to engage customers and potential customers in ways beyond marketing to them with product and services information. One of the approaches we take with the *D!gitalist* is to offer multiple points of view that surround complex issues that our target audience is trying to tackle. If we can give them content that they need to be better informed and better at their jobs, we have added value to their lives. That value builds trust, which grows to purchase consideration.
>
> We do a yearly survey of our readership. In the survey, we ask readers to compare the *D!gitalist* to other publications where they are seeking information about digital transformation. They mentioned publications like *Harvard Business Review*, *Forrester*, and *McKinsey*. That's great company to be in.
>
> We [also] find that content marketing is a great way to build credibility on a topic. You need credibility before you can successfully engage in a sales motion or even a marketing motion for that matter. Content marketing plays very effectively at the top of the funnel where a person with purchase authority or influence is gathering credible information to understand complex topics along their customer journey.

Sites such as Aon's *The One Brief*[12] are publishing upwards of three stories per theme per month, building a robust and deep library of material for readers. The site has no obvious published publication dates, which can be helpful if your content is evergreen and you need it to have an enduring shelf life on the site. If your content is timely and needs to be current and up to date, it makes sense to insert your date of publication and update any references, rates or currency information on a regular basis.

Once you and your team have established your rhythm then stick to it; plotting your resources across your year and managing budgets accordingly will ensure that you don't spend your entire resource or budget in the first few months of the financial year.

Building a strawman, or a simple calendar, as you develop your strategy will enable you to maintain your rhythm and plan specific or targeted campaigns in addition to your drumbeat output.

According to Amy Hatch, the journalistic and editorial talent behind SAP Hybris' *The Future of Customer Engagement and Commerce* (FCEC), the key to success with the site was providing high-quality, high-value articles that were produced consistently and regularly.[13] The website's accompanying newsletter has open rates of between 21 and 23 per cent, according to Michael Mischker, SAP Global VP of Digital Marketing – but most subscribers will engage with seven to eight articles on the site before choosing to subscribe. They take the time to analyse if the content is relevant and of quality and value to them before committing to signing up.

Expanding corporate storytelling

A slightly different content hub model comes from a site such as BCG. com from Boston Consulting Group. This site builds storytelling and brand journalism into the entire site – starting with its home page – integrating direct corporate headlines such as recent performance results with brand journalism and thematic content and storytelling. Whilst not technically a content hub, the *Newsroom* page of the BCG website is more magazine than PR – with pieces on trends in fintech and microfinance, tailored to the expert financial audience.

The BCG website[14] has its insight and thought leadership content front and centre – one image, and story, dominates the front page, providing multiple angles and touchpoints from one piece of research. Offering deep insight on the value of diversity, the impact of big data on corporate life, the disruption of retail, the team behind the Boston Consulting Group *Perspectives* platform is working hard to pull out engaging themes and insight from the global partnership. The stories are distributed and amplified across multiple social media platforms, building a high-quality organic audience to whom the company can communicate.

Themes driven by audience

If you want to build real empathy with your audience, ensure you are plugged into the stories that matter to them. If you look at the content hub of Duke Energy (based in North Carolina, US), called *Illumination*,[15] it promises to deliver stories that 'enlighten, inform and inspire'. Launched in 2016, the site covers stories of energy saving, energy delivery and efficiency advice, and a glimpse into the behind-the-scenes life of those who work at the company. It feels empathetic and authentic, growing out of an internal site aimed at employees. Greg Efthimiou, co-Editor of *Illumination* at launch, said that brand journalism is a way to connect directly with the company's audiences, driving growth through social media and an email distribution list.[16]

CASE STUDY

HPE Enterprise.nxt – a specialist audience

Hewlett Packard Enterprise launched its targeted *enterprise.nxt*[17] content hub to engage a specialist technical audience (namely 'IT pros') with the type of magazine content that would appeal to this niche. Content on the hub stretches from broad technical to specialist. Key to all of the content developed is accessibility, vibrancy and an engaging tone – again, the writers and editors are striving to make this content 'relatable' and relevant to those who are reading it. The site bills itself as 'the latest analysis, research and practical advice from leading experts' and boasts 1.2 million subscribers to its weekly email. Subsections are focused on topics like emerging tech, containers and innovation, and the content is developed with arresting visual images and punchy headlines to appeal to readers and subscribers. Not only is the branding subtle, but the look is stylish and classy and the tone of voice warm and engaging. Just another example of where the tech/engineering sector has stolen a march on some other industry sectors when it comes to brand journalism.

Create a clear structure

To ensure that audiences are clear on what they will be reading and seeing on your content hub on an ongoing basis, build a simple thematic structure that can flex with your business needs and requirements.

Ideally start by segmenting your audiences and identifying their business needs and requirements. Use your understanding of these needs to develop those stories that are relevant and prescient, and that link back to your core business. Aon, for instance, a professional services firm and insurer, tackles the subjects of risk and innovation, people and organizations, and capital and economics on its hub, *The One Brief*.[18] These are broad enough themes to be flexible when required, and to allow content to shift with any change in business priorities.

Build interest in your topic further – and demonstrate your curation credentials – by adding a right-hand navigation bar with further reading from within your own content hub, and consider including a further reading list of a handful of relevant articles at the bottom of each article on your site. This could be your own proprietary content, but it might also include links to external sites delivering more in-depth insight within mainstream media, such as *Fortune* magazine or the *Washington Post*.

The benefits of developing a standalone brand magazine are multiple, but the commitment in terms of time, focus and budget should not be underestimated. As with any product in today's digital environment, readers will expect an ongoing, two-way conversation and regularity of content upload. If you pursue this approach, prepare for a reasonably long-term commitment and an investment in decent content, whether you source that internally or externally. Those brands who have committed to this type of content have benefited, certainly, but they have gained senior buy-in to a serious and substantial investment to do so.

Notes

1 Hewlett Packard Enterprise (nd) enterprise.nxt. Available from: https://www. hpe.com/us/en/insights/topics.html (archived at https://perma.cc/9CW8-N3EL)

2 Ups (nd). Available from: https://www.ups.com/us/en/services/knowledge-center/landing.page (archived at https://perma.cc/9JT5-WYG7)

3   Walmart Today (nd). Available from: https://blog.walmart.com/ (archived at https://perma.cc/A5FF-5ACS)

4   IBM Perspectives (nd) IBM. Available from: https://www.ibm.com/blogs/think/uk-en/category/perspectives/ (archived at https://perma.cc/E7LT-NJPX)

5   GE Reports (nd) GE. Available from: https://www.ge.com/reports/ (archived at https://perma.cc/7U8G-7XUW)

6   Eniday (nd). Available from: https://www.eniday.com/en/ (archived at https://perma.cc/JF62-MFUH)

7   The One Brief (nd). Available from: https://theonebrief.com/ (archived at https://perma.cc/3KNQ-XGCV)

8   Johnson, A (2018) Aon shares why its content scorecard is a must, *Content Marketing Institute*, 3 August. Available from: https://contentmarketinginstitute.com/2018/08/aon-content-scorecard/ (archived at https://perma.cc/AZA2-FPPD)

9   Lazauskas, J (2015) 'We Believe in Stories': GE Reports' Tomas Kellner reveals how he built the world's best brand mag, The Content Strategist, *Contently*, 11 February. Available from: https://contently.com/2015/02/11/we-believe-in-stories-ge-reports-tomas-kellner-reveals-how-he-built-the-worlds-best-brand-mag/ (archived at https://perma.cc/JT82-8YUN)

10   Kellner, T (2015) GE Reports makes best branded content list, *GE*, 28 December. Available from: https://www.ge.com/reports/ge-reports-makes-contentlys-best-content-marketing-of-2015-list/ (archived at https://perma.cc/AP38-GNNW)

11   D!gitalist Magazine (nd). Available from: https://www.digitalistmag.com/ (archived at https://perma.cc/735F-C66P)

12   The One Brief (nd). Available from: https://theonebrief.com/ (archived at https://perma.cc/3KNQ-XGCV)

13   Papandrea, D (2017) How SAP Hybris' content marketing drives conversions, leads + ROI, *Newscred Insights*, 17 May. Available from: https://insights.newscred.com/sap-hybris-content-marketing/ (archived at https://perma.cc/7UUA-T36K)

14   BCG.com (nd). Available from: https://www.bcg.com/ (archived at https://perma.cc/86LT-X3WJ)

15   Duke Energy (nd) Illumination. Available from: https://illumination.duke-energy.com/ (archived at https://perma.cc/U2MB-USR5)

16   Boraks, D (2016) Duke Energy feature site aims to build brand, *Duke Energy*, 23 February. Available from: https://www.wfae.org/post/duke-energy-feature-site-aims-build-brand#stream/0 (archived at https://perma.cc/R4CJ-TFQ8)

17   Hewlett Packard Enterprise (nd) enterprise.nxt. Available from: https://www.hpe.com/us/en/insights/topics.html (archived at https://perma.cc/9CW8-N3EL)

18   The One Brief (nd). Available from: https://theonebrief.com/ (archived at https://perma.cc/3KNQ-XGCV)

09

Distribution and amplification: growing loyal audiences

There's no point creating content that's well researched, carefully crafted, expertly written and properly produced if it doesn't actually get consumed. Your aim is for your brand journalism to reach the audiences it is intended to be seen by. Better still, it then gathers its own momentum, having been spread across to other people's networks on your behalf by bought-in and highly engaged readers. In other words content needs distribution, and then amplification. Content needs to gain its own traction; it needs to find its own routes to audiences, and ideally expand on these as it travels.

Distribute your content well (including through paid means – see later), and the chances are you'll gain 'earned' amplification organically, as the people you initially distribute to move it on. Ideally you will kick-start the 'frictionless system of sharing' that will encourage your content to do the B2B equivalent of 'going viral'.

You can start your distribution approach by leveraging the simple power of organic engagement and sharing across your primary platforms, growing it with the support of targeted SEO and a fleshed-out approach to search. Social media amplification across channels relevant to you will boost audiences, and paid promotion will turbo-charge volumes again, and help deliver your content to very specific audiences.

FIGURE 9.1   Distributing your content

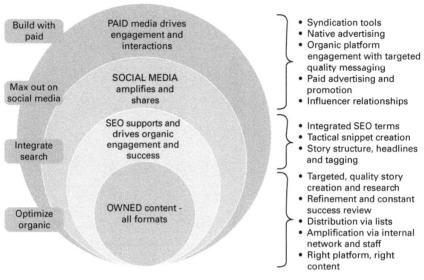

Optimize organic distribution

As recently as just a few years ago it was enough to produce high-quality pieces of content that worked by themselves and gained organic traction, but today, with very limited exceptions, you need to target specific audiences with each chosen platform early in the process, and then encourage these audiences to act as your extended distributors for you.

To do this, you must of course create content that fulfils the needs or interests of the audience and be of value to them (see Chapter 4, 'Finding the narrative'). You must also expect your audience to grow over time (aided by supplying a regular flow of content to your content hub). The beauty of optimizing organic growth is that your readers do the hard work of amplifying your content for you. But they will only do it if you meet their own expectations and fulfil their needs. Here's what you need to know to ensure organic growth happens.

Create consistently high-quality output

It's obvious, but you almost can't bang this drum enough. As author Jonah Berger wrote, in his book *Contagious: How to build word of mouth in the digital age*: 'People don't want to share things that look like ads. They don't want to look like they are a walking advertisement for a company. But they will share really engaging content, even if that content happens to relate to a brand…'. He adds: 'You need to design content that's like a Trojan horse. There's an exterior to it that's really exciting, remarkable and has social currency or practical value.'[1]

Leverage your lists

Strong, original and ongoing thought leadership and content has significantly more chance of growing organically if your initial distribution networks and mailing lists are second to none.

Since 2018 (with the introduction of the GDPR regulation that curtailed the storage of people's personal details without permission), many publishers have had to rebuild their lists from scratch. Those that already target content to largescale audiences will have already segmented their list to ensure they are carefully targeted. Having done this though, the one advantage of the regulations is that marketers can at least segment any new content on a regular basis to each of these different audiences.

The process of aligning certain pieces of content to particular lists should underline the fact your lists are powerful data sets in their own right. It's well worth analysing which are the most successful stories to bundle or deliver to certain groups.

Part of the success of a list will be how stories are initially presented in email blasts to users in the first place. Click-through rates for email are still higher than for many other distribution approaches (ranging from 6 to 16 per cent depending on which sector you are in[2]), so remember to keep newsletters tight, with the introduction and story descriptions contained within them short. Stick to a simple format, with minimal images and, of course, ensure it's optimized for mobile.

You could do worse than learning from what other B2B organizations are doing in terms of newsletter distribution. Most of the brand journalism industry leaders keep their newsletters simple, clean and effective. Make people feel they're being spammed and that's when you're giving your audience ample opportunity to opt out.

Brand journalism roundup newsletter examples from the B2B space include:

- Global oil and gas conglomerate Eni sends a three-story email (normally on broad energy topics, including renewables), each week for its brand journalism activities called the *Eniday Newsletter*.
- McKinsey distributes a weekly 'Shortlist' of its content, neatly summarized as 'Our best ideas, quick and curated'.
- Aon's *The One Brief* will often promote only one main story in its regular newsletter, focusing on one of the key stories from its content hub.
- SAP's customer service team sends out two to three selected highlights as well as contributor profiles with picture.
- *Redshift* by Autodesk delivers two key stories in its weekly roundup, with images and one promoted video.
- The *Forecast* by Nutanix has an editorial introduction followed by links to the key stories of the week.

Revise and re-surface

Not every piece of your content needs to be original, and nor does it need to be absolutely 'new' in terms of the ideas that it is encapsulating or harnessing. Any content strategy that needs volume (especially if you have developed a content hub with multiple streams of content), should always include a plan for re-surfacing older material that is evergreen in nature.

Luke Kintigh, Head of Content Distribution and Social Media at Autodesk, the company behind the online magazine *Redshift*, says most of the content it produces is surfaced more than once. 'Our strategy is not to break the news', says Kintigh. 'Our strategy is to find the white space in a trend. We are not creating a lot of real-time event coverage, it's more thought-provoking in-depth content, and a lot is evergreen.'[3]

To ensure recycled content is a booster of audiences, make sure you:

- **Establish a system for surfacing repeat content:** use your data and apply a consistent retrospective scan (after one month, three months or six months, for example), to source and discover content that can be re-posted.
- **Audit each piece:** it may well be that time references and/or any references to names or titles are now out of date or irrelevant. Consider how news events might have changed the context or any of the commentary.
- **Re-work pieces:** particularly those that are strong on numbers but probably need freshening or updating. Changing the headline, updating references, replacing imagery or key statistics or including a new interview can all revitalize a piece and give it a second bounce with new readers.

Use your staff to amplify

Never underestimate the value of one of your best amplification tools: your own staff. It can be a challenge to encourage staff members to share your content consistently to their networks, but employees are a particularly fruitful place to amplify organic content. Here is how to get started:

- **Find the evangelists:** first analyse your teams to understand who are the key thinkers and influencers in your organization. Who is sharing their story, their ideas and their writing in a successful way?
- **Share internally:** use your internal communications hub or internal newsletters to share links and ideas for stories as you push them out on social media or hubs such as Facebook Workplace.
- **Develop a toolkit:** for launches, campaigns and strategic pushes, you could consider developing toolkits incorporating template

content, messaging, images and ideas to support people's personal posting.

- **Training sessions:** share your knowledge and insight of what works well on social media to the rest of your team(s) and individuals keen to get involved. Devolve the training, record it and share it via internal collaboration tools to amplify the message internally.

- **Implement a tool:** large organizations should consider using tools such as LinkedIn Elevate, or an SaaS tool that will support multi-platform sharing for your own content internally.

- **Brainstorm sessions:** at your story-mining brainstorm sessions, encourage staff to report on how individual pieces of content have performed, and what feedback they have received when they have distributed stories.

- **Gamify the process:** encourage sharing by using gamifying where you can, building in targets and goals. Create competitions and give out rewards for successful sharing.

Integrate search

Two organizations feature regularly in this book – The World Economic Forum and SAP. It's with good reason. Both have been extremely successful in using brand journalism content for many years to drive an organic audience.

In particular, their content creation teams ensure that it's as easy as possible for content to be found by search – which means clever application of data and use of SEO (search engine optimization). These are just some of the considerations they make sure they address:

- **Writing and re-writing headlines:** the best creators think innovatively about how they frame your headlines, including using lists where possible. One tip is to include long-tail search terms where possible.

- **Deep research to deliver better topics:** easily found content has been well researched with a target audience in mind. Use Quora queries and Google searches to find how people are searching for content, to help you come up with new ideas or new thinking/ approaches.

- **Stay informed:** top-notch content creators watch the content their audience is watching, go to the events they speak at, and read the subjects they are blogging or re-posting on.

- **Newsjack:** in Chapter 2 I outlined how you can newsjack to create and deliver great story ideas. Review some of those suggestions for your own content.

- **Event coverage:** content creators review largescale events by industry (or, even better, attend them) to develop their own content. They hear what industry thought leaders are talking about and discussing and use these insights as starters for their own content.

Are your articles created with SEO in mind? Best practice includes:

- **Having a keyword focus:** choose keywords as part of your overarching content strategy – what themes are you focusing on and what areas of those themes will be a priority for you? If, for instance, the impact of 5G on telephony is a subject area you are interested in, create headers and content that reflect that search term. It's possible to build an audience, especially for your evergreen content, using long-tail search approaches like this. SAP's FCEC content hub dominates in more than 250 specialist, long-tail search terms through consistent focus on quality and commitment to key themes and topics. For more information, Neil Patel writes at length about the benefits of long-tail keywords[4] for SEO.

- **Sourcing key terms:** there are many tools out there to help you source information about topics that are trending and which are of interest to your audiences. You can find instant guidance on search terms on Google Analytics or Google Trends. Other tools such as BuzzSumo, Pulsar and Parse.ly offer a wealth of data that is limited only by knowing how to best use it to answer the questions you have. Half of the battle is knowing what questions to ask.

- **Using meta descriptions:** write a meta description that clearly identifies what's in your piece and leverages your SEO terms.

Max out on social media

National Public Radio in the United States famously created the acronym 'COPE' – or Create Once, Publish Everywhere – and it's a neat way to consider your approach to stretching your content as far as possible both on your own content hubs and on social media.

There's a very good reason why this is relevant. According to research by DemandBase and DemandGen (in their 2018 B2B Buyers' Survey Report[5]), more than half of B2B buyers say they rely on social media to research vendors and solutions. In addition to this, more than a third said they asked for suggestions and recommendations from other social network users, and specifically connected with individual thought leaders directly to ask their opinions about issues.

Before you start, you will still need to create a coherent brand story across all of your amplification channels as you seek to drive maximum returns from your high-quality journalistic content. Return to your audience personas to understand where they are, how they digest content and what platforms they prefer in the various geographies in which you wish to engage with them. It's likely also that your tolerance for risk and innovation will play an important part of which platform(s) you choose to use for your social media amplification.

Gary Vaynerchuk, CEO of VaynerMedia, a full-service advertising agency,[6] has built his own 'reverse pyramid' approach to taking content and re-purposing it for multiple platforms. His team took just one of his keynote speeches and re-purposed it into more than 30 pieces of further content for distribution on his social media channels, which subsequently reached more than 35 million views.

FIGURE 9.2 The content distribution flow

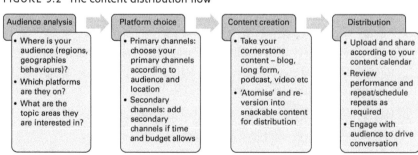

To do this yourself, each channel will need a specific approach or hook to engage your audience, whether you are creating organic posts, organic posts with ad support, or straight adverts. Our learnings on how to craft these messages include:

- **Headline refinement:** work hard on your headlines to ensure they are short, clear and punchy. Keep sentences active and use action words at the start of both headings and main text.
- **Images:** faces work well, so do clear, bold and powerful images. Don't use distant wide shots. Use charts and statistics, which work especially well on Facebook, LinkedIn and Twitter.
- **Play around with length:** the length of posts depends on your channel and will need to be tested as you build and grow your activity. Facebook posts can be kept short and sharp, but you might want to test longer posts on Instagram, potentially up to 200 words with further links to read more.
- **Trackable shortlinks:** if you are a larger brand and are distributing large amounts of content you can look into creating a 'personalized shortlink' that includes your brand name. If budget prohibits this, there are plenty of providers who can deliver shortlinks for sharing across platforms.
- **#hashtags:** where appropriate – especially for platforms such as Instagram – use all relevant and useful hashtags to build audience engagement and drive engagement with your content. If working with influencers, or named individuals with their own followers or audiences online, then @reference them also.

Create multiple assets that tap into different news lines, or pull out a statistic and create a matching graphic. Use pull quotes from a range of key people quoted or referenced in your article.

Build with paid distribution

Organic audiences will grow over a tracked period of time, but if you are in a hurry, or you have a very targeted campaign or project to promote, you will need to grow your audience using paid content distribution. Because it can be challenging building an audience from scratch, the benefit of using a paid approach is that you target audiences very tactically and then focus on growing your organic audience after that.

My main recommendation is to use a selection of channels and build them up in parallel, testing as you progress. Over-focusing on one channel is not a sensible strategy; in social media marketing, nothing stays the same for very long, so it's far better to test and learn. Remember you are building your audiences on rented platforms and you will be at the mercy of the platforms if they change or tweak their algorithms.

Don't forget to also set a clear budget before you embark on your social paid strategy. At least with testing, you can turn off the channels that don't deliver the results you need, and boost activity on those channels that do show results.

Table 9.1 shows the key platforms to consider for both organic and paid B2B growth.

TABLE 9.1   Key platforms for organic and paid B2B growth

	Detail	Activity: Organic	Activity: Paid
Facebook	54 per cent of B2B marketers use Facebook as a tool for their business and the age of the average Facebook user is rising. Best used as part of a broader organic and paid approach.	Organic reach has been declining since 2014, but the average organic reach for a Facebook post is 6.4 per cent of a page's likes – so there's still engagement to be had. Average engagement with a post (comment or share) is 3.9 per cent. Use native video if you have it, along with text and image posts; Facebook stories and FB Live are also options for B2B coverage.	Choose posts that are performing well organically and appeal to your audience and boost these posts, potentially running a number of campaigns sequentially to determine the best performer. Consider re-targeting to lookalike audiences with FB ads.

(continued)

TABLE 9.1 (Continued)

	Detail	Activity: Organic	Activity: Paid
LinkedIn	More than 550 million professional users are now active on LinkedIn globally, sharing information, news and personal updates. Use for quality brand amplification and engagement with themed brand stories.	Use your company pages to amplify your brand journalism material on a regular schedule or calendar, using either text-based content, video or live video if available. Companies like PwC, WeWork and Siemens are all using their own native versions of social video, live video or animations to deliver messaging on the platform.	Use your budget to promote specific posts to target audiences, specific people or job titles or geographies.
Instagram	The photo- and video-sharing app has a billion monthly users and benefits from the growing appeal of video and image-based content. Use it to deliver short-form versions of your thought leadership and brand journalism. Don't overlook it as simply for B2C audiences.	Use video where you can, but don't overlook text and bold imagery to draw attention to your B2B brand. Take a look at the *Economist*'s channel, GE, or the *Harvard Business Review* Instagram channels to see how to deliver intelligent content in a short-form version. Do not shy away from longer text posts accompanied by bold, arresting images. Use Stories for live events.	Use paid ads and download clickthrough promotions to share deeper material, to encourage sign-ups and downloads, or to grow subscriptions.
Twitter	You will need high volumes of social media posts on Twitter to engage your audience and drive meaningful traffic – per post engagement.	As your tweets do not reach a high percentage of the available audience, build a robust repeat schedule without over-promoting or over-repeating. Include clickable, tweetable quotes in your copy for ease of sharing, as well as adding social sharing bites to each article, video or content hub.	Create paid campaigns targeted at key audience groups.

CASE STUDY

Redshift: Building a quality audience with a targeted paid approach

Redshift by Autodesk is an online content hub that publishes high-quality brand journalism about the 'future of making'. Redshift's mission is to 'explore how products, buildings, and cities will be built tomorrow, and into the future'. Its head of content distribution and social media at Autodesk is Luke Kintigh, and in an interview for this book, he explained how, in his view, you need to build on a paid audience to grow engagement at the start of any volume content play:

> At Autodesk we aim to publish a target of three articles a week. Initially you have to use paid amplification just to start building the audience. I recommend using paid at first, but with the aim of using paid dollars to gradually convert every paid reader into a repeat reader – for instance through email, or you can get them to subscribe to your list. That person could then become your customer.

> The trick is to look beyond the numbers. At Autodesk the personas are clear in terms of the people we are trying to acquire. We are trying to use tools and data to understand our audiences – for instance, out of 10,000 views, are we reaching the people we want to influence? I think that some content marketers only think about traffic, rather than who is behind the numbers.

Other paid strategies

Broaden your reach with native advertising

Native advertising allows you to publish your brand journalism on the platforms of traditional publishers through paid agreements.

A publication like *BrandVoice* from Forbes takes editorial content from brands and publishes it within the *Forbes* magazine online. Crucially though, it's separated from the non-branded editorial content. Many other traditional publishers – the *New York Times* (T Brand Studio), *Wall Street Journal* (Custom Studios) and *Washington Post* (WP BrandStudio) are also offering this sort of service, often with in-house studios or newsrooms creating the multi-platform content for brands in close alignment to the content they are publishing for the un-sponsored section of their newspaper, website or publication.

Generally brands that are creating native advertising are looking for amplification to targeted audiences who they know will have an affinity for their messaging. By publishing on a third-party platform instead of their own, brands will benefit from both the wider network and the differentiated amplification this can offer. Many traditional publishers offer this type of placement (or a version of it), including the *Guardian* and the *Financial Times* in the UK.

Advertisers in *Forbes* include Siemens and Mitsubishi Heavy Industries, which have their own mini content hubs on the site to engage directly with the *Forbes* audience, featuring high-quality stories. The native advertising technique is similar to brand journalism, with the journalists focusing on stories that build on the intersect of the audience's interests, with the brand's focus or business priorities. It's worth noting, however, that placement and production will involve a substantially higher budget commitment than publication on your own platforms.

The rise (and rise) of influencer marketing

Another channel to consider for your brand journalism creation and amplification is the B2B influencer. There have been many question marks about the legitimacy of influencers for marketing purposes in the B2C space, but they can have a role to play in your marketing arsenal, especially with today's focus on thought leadership and one-to-many engagement.[7]

Often these people will be users or advocates of your business already – and in this instance, I am thinking of influencers who are outside of your organization, rather than internal. But as well as the more established and high-profile individuals in your industries, you might find influencers within your own company ranks who you can encourage and who will thrive with support and guidance. For more information on internal influencers, see Chapter 10 on thought leadership.

Global marketing speaker and author Neal Schaffer explained to me:

> One promising area that most companies overlook is the potential that engaging with influencers can have for your business, even if you are a B2B brand. Working with influencers in the B2B space usually is either content related (guest posting, interviews, etc) or is event related (invite to attend, moderate, or even speak at an event), but both methods can generate fantastic results for the smart companies building relationships with and collaborating together with B2B influencers for a win-win relationship.

Whilst the majority of the high-profile spend on influencer marketing of the moment is in the B2C space, there are many B2B brands who have been using influencers and specialists to engage for some time. A tactical alignment can position your brand with authentic and honest reviews, thought leadership and insight. It can also serve to help your brand with amplification of your message during a time of crisis – but this can only work if you have built a relationship and established a connection. Authentic, specialist influencers are a prerequisite; this is about depth and substance.

CASE STUDY

VMWare Influencer Network[8]

The software company has a group of highly technical, engaged and active bloggers and evangelists who write and comment on their products. The network tends to discuss highly technical information, delivering insight and helping problem-solve to a wider group of users. The VMW are community site aggregates all chat with influencers across multiple social platforms. Top influencers are 'rewarded' with access to beta tests and enhanced relationships with product teams, along with site visits.

Influencer relationships might come in a range of guises:

Hosting your content: consider using an influencer, author or journalist who is a respected insider in your space to host a podcast or video, or Q&A.

Testing your service or product: approach an influencer to consider using your product. Ensure that person is a good fit for you (both culturally and professionally)[9] and that they are open to your brand or product.

Creating content: approach B2B thinkers – internal or external – to partner on articles or pieces of content, or videos on behalf of your brand, or to become a brand 'ambassador'.

Discussing your product: you can migrate your engagement with an influencer from offline to online with round-table discussions, event attendance or speaking.

CASE STUDY
Adobe Influencer Network

Adobe has been using influencers for some time as part of its marketing mix, using experts across the breadth of the business. More than 50 influencers – including high-profile journalists, marketers, writers and bloggers – were brought to the recent Adobe Summit in 2019[10] and encouraged to post content throughout the event. 'We don't necessarily set individual influencer goals,' said Rani Mani, Head of Social Influencer Enablement at Adobe, on a recent podcast.[11] 'Program by program or department by department, there are different goals that each department has, and that each influencer contributes to in a variety of ways. Our main objective is to play to the individual influencer's strengths.'

Ultimately, any partnerships should be approached carefully, and strategically – think about high-quality, credible engagements that fit with your brand aspiration. These are people who might have knowledge and credibility within technical and specialist audiences – they may be journalists or analysts. But also look around elsewhere. You might well find other influencers engaging on *Reddit*, and on chat rooms or industry forums.

SEEKING OUT AND ENGAGING WITH INFLUENCERS

Influencers can bring life to otherwise technical content or insights. They can give a more practical, meaningful vector on your offering or product but they need to be aligned in their goals with those of your brand otherwise the relationship is unlikely to work.

Social media marketing consultant Mark Schaefer is Executive Director of Schaefer Marketing Solutions and author of, most recently, *Marketing Rebellion*, in which he espouses the importance of a new approach to marketing that is human-centred and always starts with the customer. Schaefer believes in the multiple benefits of an influencer outreach programme. When done well, he argues, they can help to grow trust by creating authentic advocacy and developing faster traction with a message. In our mistrustful world, the influencer can make content 'social proof', as well as providing brands with immediate awareness.[12]

BUILDING B2B INFLUENCER RELATIONSHIPS

Step 1: Discovery

Use social channels, internal team members, external research to find influencers and micro-influencers who are interested in or engaged with the topic you are focused on. Ensure you are working with credible, thoughtful people. Often those that are active in the online space might be journalists and analysts who already have affiliations or publications that they push their content to.

Step 2: Qualification

Work through your long list of potential influencers and analyse their depth of expertise; ensure the influencers embody your values and have a solid presence on social media. Match influencers or practitioners to the key fields you are seeking partners for. This might break down to specific divisions or groups in your organization, so specific expertise may be required across each of these groups.

Step 3: Approach

Consider why or how this influencer could be relevant to your brand. Approach in a respectful and measured way to start the conversation. Be clear from the start what your expectations are and what you will want from your influencer team. This is part of your marketing mix and, if it's their livelihood, your experts should be paid a fee for their time, experience and expertise.

Step 4: Engage

Once you have determined who you need, have approached them and got your influencers on board, you should be creative about the work you are expecting them to undertake on your behalf. This includes whether – or how – you want them to endorse your brand. Ideally this will be done in as subtle and transparent a way as possible – as with any content campaign, see this as a long-term relationship that will deliver benefits as it grows organically and reaches maturity over time. Ideally ensure your influencer sticks to his or her authentic messaging and areas of interest to maintain authenticity.

Other paid approaches

Search engine marketing: if your budget allows, and you want to deliver a tactical boost to a piece of content into a new market or audience arena, you might consider using search engine marketing for key pieces of content or groups of content in particular areas.

Syndication to publication platforms: services such as *Taboola* and *Outbrain* will take your content and post it on other websites that you can choose. The content will be marked as 'paid' or promotional, and will be posted alongside other brand content from advertisers.

Partner advertising or banner advertising: if you are really keen to drive an audience to a quality piece of content, you could always consider delivering targeted ads or ads on partner sites.

The above is by no means an exhaustive list and even as I write, some of the main social media channels will no doubt be tweaking their algorithms or changing their advertising methodology to reflect their changing business aspirations.

But the aim is unchanged: with a boost of judiciously located paid spend you can really kick-start engagement and build a powerful base from which to grow and build your outreach.

Notes

1 Wharton (2013) 'Contagious': Jonah Berger on why things catch on, *Knowledge at Wharton*, 13 March. Available from: https://knowledge. wharton.upenn.edu/article/contagious-jonah-berger-on-why-things-catch-on/ (archived at https://perma.cc/NB4L-4QEW)

2 Constant Contact (2019) Average industry rates for email as of June 2019, *Constant Contact*, 9 July. Available from: https://knowledgebase. constantcontact.com/articles/KnowledgeBase/5409-average-industry-rates?lang=en_US#compare (archived at https://perma.cc/Z9C3-ZWUF)

3 Quote from interview, carried out Friday 7 June, 2019

4 Neilpatel.com (nd) 5 Steps to building a successful organic traffic pipeline. Available from: https://neilpatel.com/blog/5-steps-to-building-a-successful-organic-traffic-pipeline/ (archived at https://perma.cc/76PH-VPY5)

5 Demand Gen (2018) 2018 B2B Buyers Survey Report, *Demand Gen Report*, 2018. Available from: http://e61c88871f1fbaa6388d-c1e3bb10b0333d7ff7aa972d61f8c669.r29.cf1.rackcdn.com/DGR_DG081_SURV_B2BBuyers_Jun_2018_Final.pdf (archived at https://perma.cc/5UKZ-KYCY)

6 garyvaynerchuck.com (2019) The Garyvee Content Strategy: how to grow and distribute your brand's social media content. Available from: https://www. garyvaynerchuk.com/the-garyvee-content-strategy-how-to-grow-and-distribute-your-brands-social-media-content/ (archived at https://perma.cc/5ML8-AFHT)

7 Weed, K (2018) The only solution to fake follower fraud is total eradication, *Marketing Week*, 18 September. Available from: https://www.marketingweek. com/2018/09/18/keith-weed-fake-follower-fraud-total-eradication/?cmpid=em~ newsletter~breaking_news~n~n&utm_medium=em&utm_source=newsletter& utm_campaign=breaking_news&eid=6199809&sid=MW0001&adg=85454879-9956-450A-B43D-B0A487FD0D56 (archived at https://perma.cc/V6HV-2DLK)

8 Troyer, J M (2017) The top 50 overall VMware influencers, *Medium*, 7 March. Available from: https://medium.com/influence-marketing-council/the-top-50-overall-vmware-influencers-7fc7ec32500e (archived at https://perma.cc/GN89-XDBR)

9 Convince&Convert (nd) How to Create a Thriving B2B Advocacy Community, Convince&Convert. Available from: https://www. convinceandconvert.com/podcasts/episodes/how-to-create-a-thriving-b2b-advocacy-community/ (archived at https://perma.cc/3ZH2-4TRH)

10 Adobe Blog (nd) Introducing the 2019 Adobe Summit Insiders. Available from: https://theblog.adobe.com/introducing-the-2019-adobe-summit-insiders/ (archived at https://perma.cc/N7EP-WYAX)

11 O'Shea Gorgone, K (2019) A B2B case study in influencer marketing: Adobe's Rani Mani on marketing smarts, *Marketing Profs*, 29 August. Available from: https://www.marketingprofs.com/podcasts/2019/41716/b2b-influencer-adobe-rani-mani-marketing-smarts?adref=nl082919 (archived at https://perma.cc/VP85-V24E)

12 Schaefer, M W (2015) *The Content Code: Six essential strategies for igniting your content, your marketing, and your business*, Grow Publishing, p 130

10

Thought leadership: insight from your people

'Thought leadership' is an over-used phrase that often promises a lot but delivers little. Much of what is called thought leadership is actually nothing of the sort – it's neither well thought out, nor leading edge. But innovative thinking that makes your people or your brand stand out is an obvious addition to your marketing and communications plan that can work especially well as content at the top of your sales funnel.

Insight and information delivered by leaders and experts who command respect in their respective fields has an impact and punch that other content does not. As a 2018 Edelman/LinkedIn survey recently found, 45 per cent of the 1,000 decision makers polled said they would invite an organization to bid on a project when they had not previously considered them, after engaging with thought leadership content.[1] Some 55 per cent also regarded thought leadership as a useful way to vet potential providers.

Innovative thinking makes your people or your brand stand out, and excellent thought leadership should be just this – clever, insightful and message-carrying in nature. As recent research from Forrester has shown, empathetic and authentic content is trusted much more than other sources.[2]

Establish your vision and outcomes

Plenty of good thought leadership isn't this at all – and even worse news is the fact that readers will recognize poor thought leadership. The same Edelman survey found only 18 per cent of the thought leadership they encountered was of 'excellent' quality.[3] Edelman found poor-quality thought leadership not only damages an organization's reputation, but damages its potential to win business too. Both statistics are clear proof that any strategy for thought leadership creation and delivery must be carefully planned. Like any type of content, success can't happen without significant time, energy and investment.

According to research by Barry and Gironda,[4] thought leaders are often described as people who can do one or more of the following:

- drive conversations around shared passions;
- champion new directions or ideas;
- harness intellectual firepower;
- provide consistent education on relevant matters;
- provoke new mindsets for addressing upcoming challenges;
- communicate with clarity how big ideas turn into reality;
- develop actionable strategies.

Those people who are described as thought leaders aren't 'go-to resources in their field of expertise' for no reason. Ideally they should be the foremost authorities on industry issues. They must have something new, or perhaps different, to say. They must also have a stature, view or experience that means they will be trusted.

Thought leadership content must serve a purpose – it could be answering customer pain points; it could also involve presenting a solution or tactic that can help audiences solve a business challenge, or be a wider narrative or 'purpose led' narrative that supports the views or beliefs of the broader business.

Whichever one of these alternatives you choose, understanding what great thought leadership should do is essentially an exercise in answering a number of important questions, reflecting the strategy development approach outlined in Chapter 3:

- Why are you creating thought leadership?
- Who are you talking to?
- What will you say?
- How will you deliver it?
- How will you sustain the flow?

Developing your talent pool

Great thought leadership can build brand engagement for your company early in the customer journey, before a real need has even emerged. As we've read, this is something that is incredibly important in B2B, especially where sales journeys can last many months or even years.

It's worth saying from the outset that in the corporate world, thought leadership does not have to originate from someone in an executive role. However, it does require someone who can build energy and engagement around their thinking. Corporate thought leaders can be grouped into the following broad segments:

Visionaries	Technicians	Reflectors
Wide-ranging ideas, broad thinkers who provide insight by tapping into the zeitgeist.	Those with technical insight, specialist knowledge and innovation.	Those people who reflect on their own experience, thinking or work to deliver advice or pull together other people's thoughts.

Skills you need to be on the hunt for won't just be good writing – and the written word is not the only format I advocate for delivering great thought leadership. Arguably the greater challenge is finding thinkers who can build sustained relationships with your target audiences. Here's how I suggest you go about this:

- **Find ready-made evangelists:** it makes utmost sense to build on those people who have already established themselves as thought leaders in your organization. If they are a specialist technical person, they may also have a ready-made network or audience passionate about their technical area. Finding them might be as simple as looking round the room, but in larger organizations identifying such people could be a much more labour-intensive operation. To help, search for prolific publishers from your organization on LinkedIn and Twitter and reach out to divisions and managers to recommend thinkers or team members.

- **Turn to your C-suite:** whilst not all CEOs will be engaging, charismatic or innovative in their thinking, there may be someone else in the senior team who you can support and encourage to become a thought leader. Look further afield than just the obvious. Seek out new and different voices that reflect the values of the organization in an authentic way. They don't have to create their own content – it may well be that you can pair them with a content producer who can interview them and turn what they say into a Q&A or blog post.

- **Grow your own:** map and analyse those of your team who have high follower numbers on their social media channels, strong engagement or successful publishing profiles. Encourage them to create more content and work with them to create narratives and streams of content that really matter to them. Nurturing talent across the organization will help drive engagement, sharing and distribution of your content. Ideally you should aim to find voices from all areas, geographies and levels that can represent your organization.

Employees hold the key

Sarah Goodall is a leading consultant on leveraging the power of employee advocacy and employee influence; she feels that too often thought leadership work is limited to the marketing department: 'We come from a culture where marketing owns the content, yet marketing – and I can say this because I am a marketer – are so far removed from the source of great content, which is employees and customers', she tells me. Sarah believes that marketers must look into the company to find the experts to create key content, as those people are the closest to the customer pain points: 'The knowledge experts are the ones that you want to identify first, and then you can start to help them build their social brands and become visible experts, not just internal, hidden experts.'

Sarah points out that expert-written content is more likely to be shared by peers than content that is from the organization directly, and that companies should be looking to find effective ways to activate their wider workforce:

> I really believe that employees hold the key to creating that human content, that brand journalism. If you start putting purpose behind the activity, and help the employee voice come out, then it's much more authentic, it will get higher conversion rates and the content will drive more traffic to your website. It is all about human-to-human contact.

Thought leadership inspiration

In addition to this ability to reflect the 'human side' of the business, what other qualities should you look for in thought leadership? Ideally our thought leadership would deliver consistent and ongoing original thinking, but in reality there are few standout leaders who can deliver authentic and sustained enlightenment in a ready-to-digest form. That said, there are some tools and questions you can ask of your thought leaders that can help with ideation:

Reference a personal story. Many of today's business leaders bring their own authentic stories to the workplace, building empathy and helping them ensure their teams and staff can relate to them. Great examples of those who have brought the personal into their professional lives include the current CEO of Microsoft, Satya Nadella. He has written and spoken extensively about his family life and its impact on him and his work. Whilst bringing this level of candour into the public domain might not suit everyone, it will help create empathy and trust.

Get involved in the global conversation. When thought leaders read industry news and imbue themselves with the sorts of wider narratives that are vexing business and governments alike, they can quickly plug into the themes that set the context for all our lives. Being familiar with foundations and charities can also ensure thought leaders add to their understanding of a topic. Seeing what content competitors and suppliers have also published can be beneficial too.

Use life events to trigger innovative thinking. Virgin Group founder Richard Branson consistently delivers original content and thinking. A technique often used by his team is to create content triggered by a particular life event – for instance, he's just seen in the New Year (time for fresh thinking); or has just welcomed a new grandchild (time to reflect); or just launched a new product (the changing nature of customer need), etc. The point is, these articles and blogs are not simply PR announcements; they are turned into stories that feel more engaging and relevant because they are woven into real life, and are full of character and personality.

Use company events to create content. If the idea of reflecting on their personal lives doesn't suit your thought leaders, events they might be more comfortable creating content around are those related to the company itself. Content should be less about pushing an event as a PR exercise, but more using it as a 'jumping-off point' to another story or personal reflection.

HOW TO USE A PRODUCT LAUNCH AS A 'JUMPING OFF' POINT

A product launch is the perfect event to consider using as a jumping-off point. To make it impactful, you could use any of the following questions as a basis from which you can develop personal product stories:

- How long did a product take to launch and who was involved?
- Where did the idea first emerge?
- How has it changed over the development period?
- Who drove that change and why?
- What did the launch team learn along the way?
- What are their personal stories?

- What challenges were encountered?
- How did you, or they, overcome them?
- How did teams who developed the new product collaborate?
- How many different teams were involved, in how many countries?
- How far did they travel to achieve this goal?

Use secondary research as a jumping-off point. If your next company event isn't for some time, it's possible to use other people's research or insight to create an alternative jumping-off point. New industry research is great, because it gives you the freedom to pull out an insight or new fact that is of interest or relevance. From here, thought leaders can build out a wider article, adding their own thinking or that of their C-suite target. A recent World Economic Forum *Agenda* blog – 'Wind farms now provide 14% of EU power – these countries are leading the way'[5] – is a perfect example of this in action. So too is another article it has produced: '7 of the world's 10 most polluted cities are in India',[6] which was based on research by the World Health Organization.

Use original research as a story base. Why use someone else's research when you can use your own? Original research is a fantastic starting point for a series of thought leadership pieces based on the findings of solid and in-depth research. Not only does it raise your organization's credentials, it is a good way to get traction across multiple platforms. In addition to hosting the main report, thought leaders have the opportunity to break it down into digestible sections or shareable images, quotes and articles. When research is original, thought leaders can legitimately appropriate the insight to contextualize wider arguments or point they want to make.

Take a personal journey or moral framework. What was your biggest failure? What have you learned during your career? When did you find yourself pushing the boundaries? How have you had to flex to succeed? Audiences love to be told the answers to these sorts of questions.

Use a passion or mission to educate. A benefit of really knowing your thought leaders well is that you can unearth potential interesting side interests or passions they might have that they are confident and articulate on. Even though their passions might only be tangentially linked to the business, opening up about something different demonstrates they have depth. Jeff Weiner, CEO of LinkedIn, posts on his social media channels about themes such as leadership, strategy and vision as well as culture in the workplace. His posts are heartfelt (sometimes only brief) and readers seldom get the sense they're being created by someone else on his behalf. They're authentic and in a human voice.

Aggregate originality. If thought leaders are struggling to come up with original research, or an angle that is radically new or different in their industry, they might consider developing thought leadership based on aggregating other people's thinking. By taking on the role of a curator of other original thinking, thought leaders can still build up a body of work they can comment on that is relevant and interesting.

Content success factors

By considering the previous advice and only producing content when it meets one or some of the criteria, your thought leadership will automatically stand a much better chance of achieving cut-through. You should also consider the following guidance when creating your own content, or working with your senior team members to help them produce their own.

1 Be authentic and heartfelt

The need to be authentic cannot be overstated. Research indicates 80 per cent of consumers say 'authenticity of content' is the most influential factor in their decision to become a follower of a brand.[7] In terms of how this translates to thought leadership pieces, the watchword is that content must try to connect – and do so in a 'human' (ie not overly corporate) voice. If there's any suspicion at all that content isn't authentic in some way then it will dilute its impact. It may well be that a blog is 'ghostwritten' after a detailed interview, or the talking points are mapped out for a podcast, but even here, it's essential all original emotion remains. Thinking must be that of the thought leader, whatever format it's delivered in.

2 Ensure leaders connect their passions with their target audience's needs

While it's possible to leave the creation of content entirely to your subject matter experts (and many organizations do), it's likely that if an expert thinks about their subject all of the time, they may not translate it in a way that readers find engaging, or which addresses problems in the here and now. So it's essential their passion connects with audiences, and does so in a coherent way.

Many senior executives have great ideas, and great insight, but they lack the time or skills to make them interesting written narratives. This is when having a marketing department, a communications team, an external agency or a professional writer can help. These people can interview your thought leaders to uncover raw, uncut, unpolished nuggets of insight that can be built on and developed into content. This is where the art of brand journalism really comes into its own – taking unrefined ideas, spotting their potential, and knowing what needs to be done to broaden them out into great stories.

NEWSROOM TIP

Look for a news peg

Journalists in newsrooms look for a news 'peg' – the reason a story is relevant for our audience at this particular moment. Great content finds a different angle or a different approach to a story that people are already discussing. If you find this difficult to do, use search trends tools, including AnswerThePublic or BuzzSumo to assess which topics are popular now, so you know how to move them on. This does not have to be linked to a major event or happening – it could simply be because there is a broad interest or resurgence in interest in a subject, theme or product.

3 Keep on posting

Regular thought leadership posting is crucial for building, maintaining and developing your audiences. If your readership enjoys your content they will come to expect that it will be delivered predictably and regularly. This doesn't mean you have to publish daily, but whatever your schedule is, ensure you stick to your planned publication dates.

4 Invite comment

IBM's *Passion Projects*[8] or Microsoft's *Research Blogs*[9] both also invite wisdom in from their crowd. The Microsoft blogs demonstrate the depth and engagement of their people with in-depth interviews that reveal the human behind their work. In the case of *Passion Projects*, articles themselves are not written by individuals per se; in most instances, their insight and thinking is delivered through interviews developed into blogs using first person quotes.

5 Choose the right format

If your CEO or other cast of thought leaders perform incredibly well on video, then take advantage of these skills and make use of this format rather than simply focusing on text output. There are exceptions, but most people are not at all relaxed or incisive on video, nor do they exude any real energy, so don't shoe-horn your thought leaders into formats they're not comfortable with. Play around though, to at least see what they like or dislike and what works best for your content.

Thought leadership comes in many guises – Microsoft Research, for instance, has developed an insightful series of podcasts interviewing a broad range of its people about their work and their broader interests.[10] Titles include broad, values-based subjects, such as 'Making the Future of Work Work for You' and 'Speech and Language: the Crown Jewel of AI'.

6 Don't do the hard sell

Given that all brand journalism has the purpose of bringing in advocates (and ultimately new business), at some point down the line the temptation can be to make thought leadership a hard-sell affair.

Remember that the main goal of effective thought leadership is to demonstrate knowledge and insight about your subject area or area of focus – and to do it without demanding a direct follow-through from your reader. Articles, podcasts or videos should simply align the personality or the brand to effectiveness in a particular arena or sector. In this way, thought leaders can support brand awareness for your organization, demonstrating that your senior people are thinking more innovatively than the competition.

As global co-head of brand and content strategy at Goldman Sachs, Amanda Rubin, says, the point of its own content is to create 'value exchanges' in the digital environment, so audiences will think more positively about the Goldman Sachs brand.[11] Goldman Sachs' website has its own *Exchanges* podcast platform that delivers wide-ranging insight from leading thinkers and advisers from the business. Titles include everything from 'What's Keeping Insurers Up at Night?'[12] to 'How is Tech Reshaping the City Skyline?'[13] These in-depth pieces are delivered on a regular and accessible platform, hosted by Goldman Sachs' Global Head of Corporate Communications, Jake Siewert.

NEWSROOM TIP
The open question

An open question is designed to deliver a full and detailed answer when you interview someone for either video or text content development. An open question will start with a 'what?', 'why?', 'how?' or 'who?', to ensure you don't receive a host of 'yes/no' answers.

Ideation and creation support

Already in this book we have discussed how brand journalism content *can* be outsourced if it saves time or improves standards. Because thought leadership is more personal in nature, some suggest this particular type of content is less suited to being outsourced. The main concern is that the 'real person' (their connection, empathy, passion) becomes obscured through the filter of another person's writing. In reality many of the world's most high-profile thought leaders will use a communications team, ghost writer or agency to support their ongoing content creation in some guise.

If you are delegating thought leadership content to internal team members, or if you are looking to use an agency to create this type of content, Table 10.1 shows a process you can follow to help you to create and deliver ongoing content that is authentic and taps into the organization's offer and messaging without compromising honest delivery and output.

TABLE 10.1 A process for thought leadership content

1	Research and ideas development	Research the environment and the work or activity of your target thinker. Develop a series of potential story ideas that you can flesh out with your interviewee or subject matter expert.
		These ideas should ideally come directly from your interviewee themselves, but sometimes – especially if they have limited time available – this can be a challenge.
		Develop a series of potential topics that can be covered and sign these off with the executive and/or her communications or PR team.
2	Questions	Once you have decided on the topics you will cover it's important to have your questions signed off by your interviewee so they can prepare properly.
		Ideally work to your article abstract or video structure (or whichever format you are choosing) to ensure you elicit the correct information in your answers.
		If your thought leadership is in video interview or podcast format then supply questions beforehand to allow your interviewee to prepare; ideally you will do the same with your text interviewees also.

(continued)

TABLE 10.1 (Continued)

3 Logistics	Ensure you set up your interview well ahead, and that it is scheduled with enough time for a real dialogue or discussion to happen.
	Leave enough time locked into the diary to give you the option to cover all areas that are relevant. This will also take the pressure off interviewees.
	Consider bundling two sets of article questions together to give you source material for additional blogs, articles or insight pieces. Make the most of the time you have.
4 Interview	Interviews to source information for writing text articles can be done over the phone or face to face. Whether you are in-house or external, a face-to-face interview is always preferable.
	When you are in the room with an interviewee it builds rapport and leaves less room for misunderstanding.
	Whether on site or on the phone, record the interview and mine it out for additional story ideas – either for your thought leadership or wider content plan.

Depending on the aims and outcomes sought for each piece of content, once created, distribution of insight pieces can be via the individual's social channels or website, as well as via the corporate sites and channels, amplified across your corporate social channels.

You should also consider third-party sites for publication or re-publication of text articles, such as *Medium*,[14] that can help amplify your output, as can publishing or syndicating to sites such as *Forbes, Inc* and *Huffington Post*. Ultimately, selling is a human-to-human experience, and tapping into the rich seam of thinking inside your organization – no matter how large or small – will help build longer-lasting relationships with your target audiences.

Notes

1 Edelman (2019) 2019 B2B Thought Leadership Impact Study, *Edelman*, 5 December. Available from: https://www.edelman.com/research/2019-b2b-thought-leadership-impact-study (archived at https://perma.cc/7SLF-DVLJ)

2 Ramos, L (2017) Peer stories and credible data attract and engage B2B buyers use short-form interactive content to capture customers' attention, *Forrester*, 7 September. Available from: https://on24static.akamaized.net/event/16/73/65/8/rt/1/documents/resourceList1528136053847/forrestercomplimentaryreportpeerstoriesandcredibledata1528152417373.pdf (archived at https://perma.cc/6E6G-HW53)

3 Edelman (2019) 2019 B2B Thought Leadership Impact Study, *Edelman*, 5 December. Available from: https://www.edelman.com/research/2019-b2b-thought-leadership-impact-study (archived at https://perma.cc/7SLF-DVLJ)

4 Barry, J M and Gironda, J T (2017) Operationalizing thought leadership for online B2B marketing, *Industrial Marketing Management*, **81**, pp 1–22

5 Fleming, S (2019) Wind farms now provide 14% of EU power – these countries are leading the way, *World Economic Forum*, 6 March. Available from: https://www.weforum.org/agenda/2019/03/wind-farms-now-provide-14-of-eu-power-these-countries-are-leading-the-way/ (archived at https://perma.cc/K33P-B42U)

6 Thornton, A (2019) 7 of the world's 10 most polluted cities are in India, *World Economic Forum*, 5 March. Available from: https://www.weforum.org/agenda/2019/03/7-of-the-world-s-10-most-polluted-cities-are-in-india/ (archived at https://perma.cc/CR9M-P2US)

7 Sweezey, M (2015) 5 content engagement questions answered, *Slideshare*, 16 December. Available from: https://www.slideshare.net/MathewSweezey/5-content-engagement-questions-answered (archived at https://perma.cc/Q4KM-E894)

8 IBM Passion Projects (nd) Available from: https://www.ibm.com/thought-leadership/passion-projects/ (archived at https://perma.cc/AJT8-SE3V)

9 Microsoft (nd) Microsoft Research Podcast. Available from: https://www.microsoft.com/en-us/research/blog/category/podcast/ (archived at https://perma.cc/8Y5X-4DJN)

10 Ibid

11 Baker, D (2017) How finance brands like Goldman Sachs use content to build trust and win customers. contently, *Contently*, 20 April. Available from: https://contently.com/2017/04/20/goldman-sachs-build-trust-win-customers/ (archived at https://perma.cc/6CSR-T2PR)

12 Siegel, M (2019) Episode 124: What's keeping insurers up at night? *Goldman Sachs*, 7 May. Available from: https://www.goldmansachs.com/insights/podcasts/episodes/05-07-2019-mike-siegel.html (archived at https://perma.cc/XB66-U54T)

13 Garman, J (2019) Episode 120: How is tech reshaping the city skyline? *Goldman Sachs*, 1 April. Available from: https://www.goldmansachs.com/insights/podcasts/episodes/04-01-2019-jim-garman.html (archived at https://perma.cc/7GD9-8XRT)

14 Medium (nd). Available from: https://medium.com/ (archived at https://perma.cc/XW24-39BH)

11

Measuring impact: building a metrics framework

We have covered how to develop and distribute your brand journalism content for maximum impact, but successfully tracking the results remains a real challenge. If you are lucky enough to work with an end-to-end content management system, or an integrated single channel, then your measurement will be relatively straightforward, but the reality tends to be a mixture of various channels, tools, and a lot of data that you need to make sense of.

As well as the complexity of multiple channels of content, there's also the challenge of mapping where your content ends up. Sharing and distributed networks mean we cannot always track how our content and messages end up landing with our audience. Measurement needs to be undertaken using a bespoke solution, developed specifically to work for one brand, or brand channel. It doesn't have to be complicated if you are dealing with limited paths of activity, but it must be consistent, and tracked against time to demonstrate longer-term trends, as well as short-term successes or engagement.

Your focus on metrics should be driven by the specific goals you are targeting and judged accordingly. Often marketers are in a short-term cycle, looking for instant results from posts and content upload – you can certainly use key metrics to measure that type of activity, but it won't give you the full picture, not least because your content (if carefully and strategically targeted to your audience's needs) will keep on having an impact on aspects of your strategy such as SEO well after it is uploaded and shared.

> The content teams of tomorrow are not just top-of-the-funnel sales enablement teams. They are not just SEO-focused teams driving brand awareness. They are not just customer support organizations, managing how-to videos or customer events. Tomorrow's content teams are the experts in delivering audience value at every stage of the customer's journey.
>
> *Robert Rose, content marketing author and*
> *Founder of The Content Advisory*[1]

Any measurement approach must assess success as you see it, based on your own precise content goals, as outlined when you developed your strategy and approach to content creation. I would recommend you take a broad, holistic approach to measuring your results, and assessing the data. As content strategist and consultant Rebecca Lieb writes:

> Measuring only for sales and leads – or simply relying on volume or vanity metrics such as 'likes' and 'views' that contain little business value – undermines and devalues investments in time, media, employees, technology and vendor relationships.[2]

Investing for the long term

Marketing expert Michael Brenner outlines his approach to ROI in an interview for this book, taking as his starting point the concept of content marketing as an annuity – something you invest in for a longer period of time that delivers value at the end of a cycle:

> If you publish consistently, like a publisher does, you see an increase in traffic over time and it's a compounding increase in return. If I write customer-focused content that can attract an audience of people and then if I can engage them more deeply in my brand, perhaps with gated offers, newsletter subscriptions, or a course, or book, then I can generate leads that can ultimately convert to revenue. That's an annuity, it's a financial asset. In order to get that annuity, that return on investment at a compounded rate of return, you have to invest consistently.

Mitsubishi Heavy Industries has integrated its brand journalism across a range of its global communications on its owned sites (on its corporate website, *MHI.com*, as well as on its content hub, *Spectra*[3]) alongside native advertising and content partnerships on global publishing platforms such as *Forbes*, the *Wall Street Journal* and the *Financial Times*. There are multiple approaches to measurement of this type of content. MHI's global content activity is supported by local, discrete campaigns and paid activations where needed. Thought leadership material on *Spectra* is focused on 'making the customer smarter' by offering insight on relevant subjects such as global manufacturing, the changing nature of the workplace and broad energy and environmental challenges. Where possible, media relations opportunities support campaigns and activations that are running on paid and earned channels.

By closely integrating marketing and communications planning, Global Marketing Communications Director Dan Lochmann is ensuring all content and stories are working hard to build brand awareness, whilst also being leveraged (as part of lead generation and conversion material) further down the sales funnel:

> It's important that you are very clear on the objectives for your content from the start and that those objectives tie closely to your business strategy. If the business objective is to rapidly globalize a company, for instance, then you need to start communicating that in a global way. For MHI, we want to go deep into the story of what we do, what we produce, and content is a perfect way of doing that.

> In terms of measurement, we need to be focused on outcomes that deliver a strong return on our investment. For me, if I can prove that what I would call a 'top of funnel' piece of content, a piece of thought leadership, has engaged a customer who has then gone through the customer journey and in the end bought an MHI product or recommended one, that is perfect return on investment. But, at the same time, you are also building reputation [with that content] and brand value.

No silver bullet

What's clear is that there is no simple way to solve the measurement challenge. The modern marketing landscape is a complex one, as noted by Dzamic and Kirby,[4] who wrote about the 'MarTech tsunami', with thousands of operators already in the space and more to come. This fragmentation of the environment has led to a massive variety in measurement techniques and approaches, with none providing a catch-all solution that works for each client. As IBM stated in their report *2019 Marketing Trends*, we are seeing the emergence of *Marketer 4.0: the tech-savvy martecheter.*[5]

My experience is that each software provider believes its platform or solution can measure everything you need as an agency or client – but none has ever delivered. Ultimately we find ourselves in a situation where we must 'pick and mix' results to fit our aspirations or outcomes to get anywhere near a true picture of return on investment, or perhaps more explicitly, a 'return on objectives'.[6]

The solution is to develop a hybrid approach to measurement that will capture what it is you are trying to achieve with your various audiences. Our view would be that 'less is more' – be clear about what you want to measure and why, and distil that to as few measures as possible.

Start with your goals, and for each activity or campaign choose a handful of metrics and measure against those; review and update your metrics to your chosen KPIs on a regular basis.

Organic story success

You can measure everything, sure, but not all the data you measure will be relevant, and – if you're not careful – you will end up heading down multiple measurement routes. Paid campaigns will deliver refined results that can demonstrate information ranging from who digested your content, where and how much you paid for each engagement across your chosen paid platform or execution. Ongoing organic engagement can be more complicated to measure, and much of your brand journalism may sit in this organic space with little or no paid support.

For Melanie Deziel, former journalist, founder of StoryFuel, and adviser to many leading global organizations on content strategy, it's important to measure brand journalism in a different way. In an interview for this book she explained:

Many times the instinct is to measure content and storytelling initiatives in the same way we measure our ad campaigns, and that often falls short. Our content, in its consumer-facing form, is more like journalism, and so we should try to measure it in similar ways to how other content creators measure their stories. This means we likely focus less on conversion metrics like clicks or sales, and focus instead on more awareness and engagement metrics that signal our content is reaching our intended audience and causing them to pause and spend time with us. I'd recommend looking at things like reach, views, engaged time, social engagement, comments, replies, and other indicators of audience approval.

In any case, it's absolutely key to have a conversation about measurement and key performance indicators before starting any content initiative to ensure that everyone is on the same page, that we're optimizing the content for the intended goal, and that we have the infrastructure in place to measure the appropriate metrics.[7]

The World Economic Forum's digital editorial team measures and maps story performance every weekday during the internal review meeting and daily editorial meeting. Trends are also measured at weekly review meetings and strategy sessions.

This is an opportunity to understand which stories have 'travelled through the network' and been successful with the target audiences. Topics that are popular can be focused on in more detail; approaches and sentiment that are successful with audiences (for instance, optimism and positivity) can be logged. Formats that work well with audiences can be tracked.

Key to the success of the Forum's brand journalism and approach to volume publishing is this constant, close monitoring of the output and tweaking of the system and content/topics accordingly. It isn't feasible for everyone to spend this type of time and resource commitment on topics and themes, but a regular (weekly or monthly) review can serve the purpose of surfacing the best editorial themes for your target audiences.

Individual stories: what do you measure?

You can learn a lot from your organic success and metrics if you are not supporting your brand journalism with paid engagement across your social and search channels:

- **Topic success:** is one particular topic or area of discussion more successful than others?

- **Individual influencers:** are specific people in your team gaining more traction with their content? Is that down to topic, or network and sharing capability?

- **Dwell time:** do certain articles pull people in for longer? Can you learn anything in terms of either topic, writing style or content format as a result?

- **Comments, likes and shares:** what content (format, topic) is getting engagement either on your hub or on your social? What are people saying and are they developing some quality discussion?

- **Viewing time:** which videos are being viewed and shared multiple times across your channels? How many are dropping off after the five- or ten-second mark, versus a full view?

> Content is the means, not the ends. The goal isn't to be good at content. The goal is to be good at business because of content.
>
> *Jay Baer, Convince & Convert*[8]

Measurement throughout the customer journey

Measurement simply for awareness may not be enough for your organization or for clearly demonstrating ROI on brand journalism. Another approach is to match your results to the stage at which your content is 'working' within the customer journey. That might start with growing awareness, and move through building interest, growing trust and encouraging a sale or conversion – with brand journalism content you can continue to measure results and ROI post-sale, when advocacy remains important.

TABLE 11.1   Measurement throughout the customer journey

Stage in customer journey	KPIs: What is the role of our content or stories?	Metrics
Awareness	Our content needs to REACH the right people	• Views of specific pages, articles and videos (including dwell time) • Overall direct traffic to your website • Earned media mentions • Audience growth rate across owned social media platforms • Article reach on social media platforms
Interest	Content needs to ENGAGE people in order to build brand recognition	• Engagement rate: article/post/podcast/video shares and comments • Website: time on page, page views per visit, bounce rate • Social media post-engagement: likes, comments, clicks to site, social shares • Social share of voice: comparison with key competitors or campaigns • Social follower growth across all platforms
Consideration	To become a real consideration, brands need to prove they UNDERSTAND a person's needs and beliefs	• Email subscriptions and engagement rate • Conversion rates and click-through rates • Blog subscriptions, podcast subscriptions, video channel subscriptions • In-page surveys on brand sentiment
Intent	To build trust, brands and individuals must SHARE values, beliefs and expectations	• Key page visits on website – subsequent journey through site • Article and content item views, comments, shares • Time on site, time with specific articles, bounce rate
Evaluation	To make a sale, brands need to CONVINCE people of their value	• Ongoing and repeat traffic to key pages on website/content hub • Landing page downloads • Webinar and event sign-ups (offline and online)

(continued)

TABLE 11.1 (Continued)

Stage in customer journey	KPIs: What is the role of our content or stories?	Metrics
Purchase	Brands need to REASSURE people they've made the right decision by exceeding expectations through actions	• Online sales • Tracked sales conversions (via your CRM) • MQLs passed to sales teams
Post-purchase	Brands need to NURTURE this new relationship using empathy	• Content served to returning visitors • Reviews and community comments • Ongoing engagement activity on social media such as likes, comments, shares • Continued article/content shares, comments, actions

Marketing automation and measurement tools can save you time and effort. Often posting and monitoring tools (such as Buffer or Hootsuite) include analytics dashboards to allow you to measure all of these metrics and more; social media sites also supply all the data you need. If you don't have subscriptions to these tools then build spreadsheets to track and analyse your numbers.

CASE STUDY

Red Hat

The $3 billion software company Red Hat is a leader in the content marketing field; over the last few years, the company's global director of content, Laura Hamlyn, has driven the growth of a broad team creating content assets for the senior management team, the website and sales teams. She told me:

> Our approach depends on the purpose of the story and the measurability of the content type. If it's to create awareness, we can measure brand affinity before and after people engage with our content. With videos, we can also measure view completion and we can also measure subscribers to channels. With our podcast, we measure time spent listening (completes) and downloads and subscriptions. We can also measure sharing and social

sentiment. My favourite use of social is to share relevant content, and it's such a great feeling to see fans sharing our content. They actually recommend it.

We believe evergreen content and campaign content can work together well. For example, organic traffic to our website actually converts over time and creates some of our most valuable leads. We have increased the value of organic site visitors by 105 per cent year over year from 2018–19.

Our teams have aligned to messaging via what we call 'sales conversations'. These are themes we identified via research that our customers and prospects have identified as challenges/opportunities for their business.

We align with these themes across all of our marketing teams so sales, marketing, and our prospects and customers are all exposed to the same terms and concepts. Evergreen content builds trust, educates, and becomes a reliable source of information from day to day or month to month. Campaign content is more dynamic and fluid and can serve to create brand awareness via paid media, or function as a call to action, telling the prospect what action to take next. As our data and MarTech gets more advanced, we can personalize any of this content dynamically to reflect our customer and prospects goals and user profiles.

A broader measurement framework

Some will want to take a broader approach to measurement of success, especially if the aspiration is for the building of longer-term brand awareness. In her book, *Content: The atomic particle of marketing*, Rebecca Lieb outlines a compass approach to measurement that integrates a series of potential business outcomes that are broader than simple marketing or communications outcomes or funnel/journey metrics.

Broadly speaking this approach measures wider business impact of content, including:

- **Brand health:** a measure of attitudes, conversations and behaviours directed towards the brand within communities of potential customers or clients.

FIGURE 11.1   The business value of content strategy

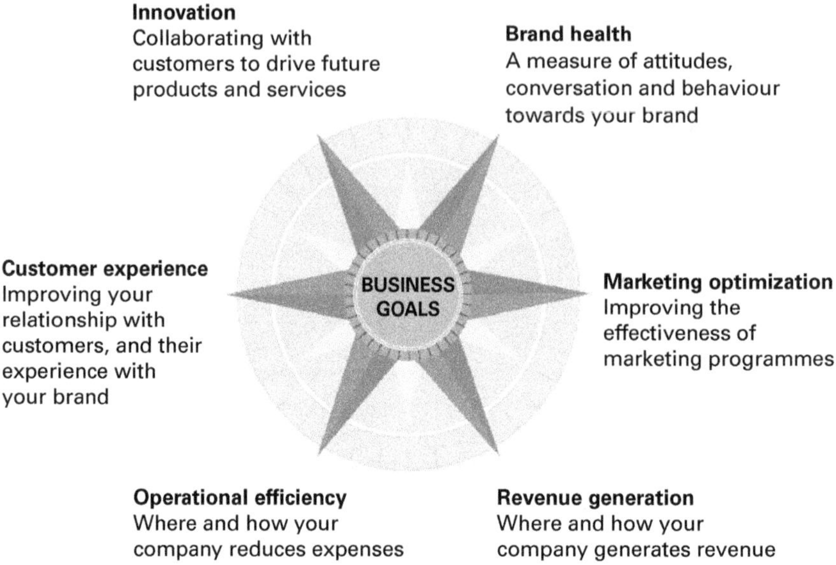

Innovation
Collaborating with
customers to drive future
products and services

Brand health
A measure of attitudes,
conversation and behaviour
towards your brand

Customer experience
Improving your
relationship with
customers, and their
experience with
your brand

BUSINESS
GOALS

Marketing optimization
Improving the
effectiveness of
marketing programmes

Operational efficiency
Where and how your
company reduces expenses

Revenue generation
Where and how your
company generates revenue

Reproduced with kind permission of Rebecca Lieb.[9]

- **Marketing optimization**: an umbrella term encompassing activity that supports wider marketing campaigns or outreach.

- **Revenue generation:** with a complex sales journey it's often difficult to track precisely where a lead has converted – is it the last-touch piece of content, or the previous four engagements with content that you measure? Direct statistics can be gathered further along the sales journey from measurable activity such as collateral downloads, gated content engagement and webinar sign-ups.

- **Operational efficiency:** streamlining production to deliver operational efficiency in certain marketing areas.

- **Customer experience:** content can demonstrate value in the realm of customer support and service, a significant cost centre in most organizations.

- **Innovation:** content can be used to solicit ideas and engagement and therefore contribute to broader organizational goals.[10]

CASE STUDY

Tata Consultancy Services, Digital Empowers

Abhinav Kumar, Chief Marketing and Communications Officer at Tata Consultancy Services, has seen the broad benefit of the purpose-led content that TCS has delivered on its content hub, *Digital Empowers*.[11] As he explained in an interview, it's not just about simple metrics:

> The point is to engage the community, analysts, investors and others – and ultimately the benefit is demonstrated when we take soundings through our brand audits. There are many things you can measure but this field is both a science and an art. There is the science part – where measurement is key – and data has made that easier, but there also has to be room for instinct and gut layered onto that. We created short-form social videos for many of our stories on *Digital Empowers* and our frontline sales force has access to those. Many of them use these videos at events or if they are talking to the customer they will use those as part of their presentation.
>
> I have spoken to many people about this over the years. What they say is, when you're having a commercial conversation with a customer and you start the conversation with these stories, it creates a very different engagement and connection with that customer. It appeals to their emotions and it helps also position us as a responsible company that is doing good for society and that's an important concern for all businesses.

Stretching the value

Original content is an investment in terms of money and time, so it's important to ensure your material works as hard as possible within your organization. Top-of-funnel thought leadership or brand journalism content can be re-worked as sales and lead-generation material. For instance, aggregation of blog content into white papers, reports or insight papers for distribution via email or printed for live events.

Media relations and outreach

Often brand journalism content at the top of the funnel will be digested by numerous audiences (and paid promotion can obviously

FIGURE 11.2   Content supporting wider communications and sales outreach

target key audiences if you wish to get their precise attention). Ask the following questions as you create your brand journalism:

- Have you been liaising with your PR team to map your content against broader communications aspirations and campaigns?
- Have you delivered leads or pick-ups or any coverage from your brand journalism?
- Have you briefed your brand journalists to look for great news lines that can be offered to the PR team to build a media relations campaign or interest?

Ideally you will be working closely with the PR team to dovetail your PR activity with your publication and gain maximum traction from that. This can be as simple as scheduling brand journalism story publication at the time of a key global event (for instance, a global political event on sustainability or the UN Sustainable Development Goals).

Lead-generation material

Sales teams who are looking for specific leads can often reference brand journalism and published stories. Success of key articles can guide decisions on what audiences are interested in and might respond to.

Account-based marketing research and collateral

Targeted, quality ABM activity is supported by deep research and high-quality content. You can use your brand journalism stories to support your ABM campaigns as a jumping-off point for additional material, or re-purpose content you already have with a specific target customer in mind. Content hubs can be used to house your ABM material, with targeted paid or organic social media content amplifying your targeted storytelling.

Investor and analyst relations collateral

Your high-quality content can be aggregated or re-worked with minimal effort into longer-form investor or analyst material that can be digitally delivered to key targets, or printed for distribution at sales meetings or live events where key influencers, partners or analysts are in attendance.

There is no one simple solution to measurement of your brand journalism assets – there are multiple tools and approaches and that situation is only likely to become more complicated. There are enough examples from the market, however, to demonstrate that leaders in the field are developing and deploying hybrid approaches that successfully measure activity and success to demonstrate ROI internally. Ideally you will review and test your approach frequently as circumstances, tools and targets change, to enable your brand journalism stories to deliver both in the short term and from a longer-term point of view.

Notes

1 Rose, R (2019) Your 2020 mission: a unified strategy for content in your marketing, *Content Marketing Institute*, 28 January. Available from: https://contentmarketinginstitute.com/2019/01/unified-content-marketing/ (archived at https://perma.cc/N2YG-46LD)

2 Lieb, R and Szymanski, J (2017) *Content – the Atomic Particle of Marketing: The definitive guide to content marketing strategy*, Kogan Page Publishers, p 165

3 Spectra (nd) Available from: https://spectra.mhi.com/ (archived at https://perma.cc/6HDN-7PZK)

4 Dzamic, L and Kirby, J (2018) *The Definitive Guide to Strategic Content Marketing: Perspectives, issues, challenges and solutions*, Kogan Page Publishers, p 193

5 IBM (2018) 2019 Marketing Trends. IBM, December. Available from: https://www.ibm.com/downloads/cas/RKXVLYBO (archived at https://perma.cc/HMM2-9BJM)

6 Silvers, J (2007) Return on Objectives (ROO), *juliasilvers.com*, 27 October. Available from: http://www.juliasilvers.com/embok/return_on_objectives.htm (archived at https://perma.cc/7EYH-TFDG)

7 Email interview direct to author, 24 June 2019

8 Baer, J (nd) A field guide to the 4 types of content marketing metrics, *Convince & Convert*. Available from: https://www.convinceandconvert.com/content-marketing/a-field-guide-to-the-4-types-of-content-marketing-metrics/ (archived at https://perma.cc/F4N5-4AHS)

9 Lieb, R and Szymanski, J (2017) *Content – The Atomic Particle of Marketing: The definitive guide to content marketing strategy*, Kogan Page Publishers, p 166

10 Ibid, p 181

11 Digital Empowers (nd). Available from: https://digitalempowers.com/ (archived at https://perma.cc/XC4S-FXC3)

12

Bringing your newsroom to life

By now you will have a grasp of the role brand journalism can play in your content marketing, what stories your company can tell and how to go about publishing and creating your content, as well as distribution challenges and processes to deliver audience success. You have the strategy, the plan and, we hope, the resources – now you just need to make it happen.

Brand journalism is not a quick-hit approach to marketing success; it's part of an increasingly interesting and accessible set of tools that the modern marketer can leverage to build brand awareness and get a company noticed. If your budget can stretch to a large spend on internal staff then that's a great place to start; if not, there are other approaches to making your content happen.

> There are plenty of jobs for journalists nowadays, they're just not in journalism anymore.
> *Mark Jones, Head of Digital Content, World Economic Forum.*

Finding the smarts

As we read in Chapter 4 on developing your narrative, there are various ways that companies are choosing to create content, whether outsourcing it, developing it in-house, or blending the two approaches. Whichever way you choose to create your brand journalism approach, people, as ever, are crucial.

If you want to create a newsroom, it makes sense to bring in journalists to support you with this aim. Those who have worked at the coalface producing minute-by-minute news – whether text, online, video or radio news – have a true understanding of what it takes to tell a story effectively and efficiently, often with limited resources. If your output does not warrant having a dedicated team of journalists, think about using freelancers, or recruiting people who have journalistic attributes – look for inquisitive, smart and bright writers that you can support and grow as internal 'journalists' of your own. You can also 'grow your own' team of resourceful and inquisitive writers from your internal staffing; increasingly it's about finding team members who are happy to take on technical and data-mining skills, alongside those more traditional writing and story development abilities.

Outsourcing of content

Some organizations, especially larger, global companies with disparate teams and a range of products, use external agencies to create content for them. Many of those people I have interviewed for this book use freelance teams, or have longstanding relationships with one or two agencies.

If you choose to use an external agency for your brand journalism creation, here are my thoughts on what needs to be in place to deliver success from that relationship:

Set the tone: the first few pieces of content the agency creates for you may not be spot-on in terms of tone of voice. Learning to speak a brand's language – in all of its layers, and with all of its nuances – will take time.

Iterate: test and learn as you go, and flex your approach in turn. Ask to try different writers or producers if those you are working with at first aren't working for you or your content.

Link communications with content: content marketing and brand journalism can only benefit from being closely mapped to your PR and media relations campaigns; both will benefit from being linked.

Build a process: set up a regular commissioning and delivery process with your agency; consistency and routine will build efficiency, especially if you are creating large volumes of content across multiple platforms.

Map the red flags: be clear from the start where the issues might lie with certain narratives, commentaries or viewpoints.

Long-term commitment: as the agency and your team get deeper into the content, the messaging, and get to know the personalities and people of their client more intimately, the content will always improve.

Keep innovating: it's important to experiment with new approaches, especially in such a changing environment as that of digital marketing.

Insist on a consistent team: ideally your agency will commit a number of named writers to your account, as well as the client team, thereby ensuring that you maintain consistency of flow and approach.

The perfect team

Whether you recruit an agency that develops a team for you or your brand, or recruit and manage a team internally, you need to recruit the right range of skills. The team members you need will be determined by your strategy and approach to content creation – for instance, if you are curating more than you are creating your needs will be different from a company building and posting 100 per cent original material.

One approach to team structure involves segmented functions working to the vision of an Editor in Chief. The skills can be amalgamated into fewer team members, or supplemented with freelancers if your headcount is limited.

Reflecting the newsroom structure

We don't all have unlimited budget to hire multiple people to drive and manage content. The key team member that you need is your

FIGURE 12.1 Outline newsroom structure

Editor/Editor-in-Chief		
Editorial board: flexible team, might include communications teams, sales, PR, marketing		
Writing	**Video and visuals**	**Social media**
Writers – generalist, niche or industry or vertical focus Freelance commissioners Subbing and review team	Video creation: filming, tool management and/or editing Post-production including graphics (flat, animated, 3-D), animation etc	Social media post-creation Graphics and post-production Data analysis and review
Strategy development, quality control and cross-team data analysis		
Financial management / Managing editor / staffing and recruitment		

version of the Editor in Chief to manage and drive all your content and coverage.

Around that key role, there are other tasks that need to be done that can be fulfilled by freelancers, internal team members, or agency staff. All newsrooms are different, but here are some of the roles that you might find in such an operation:

Editor/Editor in Chief: in a traditional newsroom, these senior journalists decide how a news operation prioritizes its news output (what it wants to publish), what the key stories are and which narratives are worth pursuing given what the audience wants and likes. They coordinate the resources to decide where the focus will be, and which stories should be covered by which teams.

Reporters/writers: these are the journalists themselves on the frontline, gathering the story information and pulling together articles, long-form features, infographic and video or graphic scripts.

Subs: writers and subs will review the content of your writers and reporters, ensuring it fits the brief, is well written and reflects the tone and approach of the brand. This is also the quality control for your output. You may choose to have a team to review all pieces before they are published – sometimes called 'final eyes'.

Producers: producers might turn their hand to many pieces of editorial work in the newsroom. They might be creating and posting a range of social media content created from your brand journalism stories or they might be editing footage, sourcing information, source imagery or researching an infographic.

Data teams: with the sheer range and complexity of platforms, approaches, formats and metrics available to us today, a data analyst and a social media expert (whether in-house or outsourced) are a crucial part of your team.

The need to nurture your internal talent to be storytellers where possible, with additional journalistic support, is a common thread amongst those brand journalists I have spoken to.

Melanie Deziel founded StoryFuel, an agency working with organizations to tell their own stories more effectively; interviewed for this book she explains how she advises her clients to structure their teams:

> It's important for brands to remember that storytelling is a skill that often requires specialized talent, not unlike the technologists and technicians they likely have internally developing their own products. Often, the first step is to bring in the right talent from the worlds of journalism, communications, and other creative fields to bring the right skills in-house.
>
> After that, I always encourage brands to look internally to their own talent and experts, to see how we might help them share their stories. Everyone has what I call their 'first content language', or the format that they prefer to communicate in, whether it's speaking, the written word or something else. If we can take an internal expert, and pair them with a talented storyteller, then we can get that expert to share their experience in a natural way and have the storyteller reframe that in the most useful format for the intended audience.

Hire the right journalists

Creating a brand journalism team is not as easy as just hiring a few journalists; it's important to take on team members who understand which skills they need to leverage in the business content world, and which habits it's best to leave behind in the newsroom.

Most journalists who have spent any substantial amount of time in a deadline-driven environment are used to fitting into a production system; they become adept at working in systems where process and detail focus is necessary to generate stories and consistent coverage. That ability to produce regular, high volumes of content under time pressure is a skill that non-journalists sometimes struggle with.

However, not all journalists fit naturally into the corporate world. Some will not fit comfortably with new roles which take them away from editorial independence, into a situation where they are paid by a brand that will have a product or service to sell.

Mark Jones is a former journalist himself, and is now Head of Digital Content at the World Economic Forum, which has a team of experienced journalists at the heart of its publishing operation, and brings in additional agencies and freelancers to support that central team:

> Being able to get audiences to read what you've written, to listen to what you've said, to watch what you've produced is something that almost all organizations now are having to learn how to do, and no organization outside the media world is really a natural at that kind of activity. You need people with agile minds.
>
> We're all busy, there are massive numbers of distractions around in the world – what is the gem within this content that will make it catch on? Some journalists are above all that and don't think it's a worthy thing to do. Others are intrigued by that challenge.

Data and project management skills

In today's content creation team you will need access to analysts or experts who can work with all of your data (across social media and content development and sharing) to understand and optimize performance of campaigns or story sharing. You will also want to recruit team members who are flexible and open to learning about new platforms and tools as we see so many come and go in the content marketing space. They need to analyse which will work and which is appropriate at any given time.

According to research by Altimeter[1], the majority of content creators use website analytics as their primary source of information to determine content strategy. The most commonly used data sources for content creators and commissioners are:

- website analytics;
- customer surveys and reports;
- social media metrics;
- customer service and call centre records;
- third-party databases;
- CRM systems.

At the software giant Red Hat, Global Director of Content Laura Hamlyn has built an editorial team that coordinates wider content marketing activity. This internal marketing communications team acts as a hub for all marketing content activity. She tells me:

> We provide core resources that global teams can use to serve as an extension of our team. Our internal team knows the business intimately, and we form relationships with our marketers, sales teams and subject matter experts. That gives us a real advantage in that we can quickly get to relevant ideas that might take agencies a little longer to develop. My team likes the model because if they know the subject matter well, creative ideas come all the time. I also hire journalists, systems thinkers, researchers, PhDs and academics, athletes, bilinguals, data nerds. I love finding people who have the patience to think deeply about a topic and research it. A writing team should be eclectic. Especially as we think of connecting back-end content strategy, front-end content strategy, story development, transcreation, and data analytics. All of these things happen on our team. This team alignment provides a consistent brand voice which is critical for our business as a trusted, innovative tech brand.

So it's not simply about recruiting the right person with the right skills – as ever with your team members it's as much about attitude as anything else. According to Dietmar Schantin of the Institute for Media Strategies,[2] the modern newsroom needs:

- People who are willing to learn and change.
- Those who are 'flexi-storytellers': 'Digital media and new formats provide an endless repertoire of tools to tell stories in a compelling way.' Schantin adds: 'The goal is to develop an editorial department with a storyteller-with-new-tools mentality.'
- Staff who have an analytics mindset and a focus on the audience.

Supported by technology

As a brand journalist you will need to leverage – and continue to review – marketing technology tools within the entire span of work that you do. There is no point creating content and not getting it to the right audiences, or delivering the outcomes that you need. Your brand journalism 'MarTech stack' (group of software components) will be crucial at every stage of content strategy, creation, delivery, sharing and monitoring. You might be in the lucky position of having such a large volume of content, and the size of operation that means you can create your own editorial insights engine or tool to determine your content success, but many of you will need to purchase a tool, or use a free tool at each stage of the process.

There is a mind-boggling array of marketing technology tools out there on the market, and the details regarding this range are beyond the scope of this book. There are available a range of free options in each of these categories and it is by no means always necessary to pay for an enterprise-grade toolkit until you are dealing with high volumes of material or content.

TABLE 12.1 Brand journalism technology tools

Content analysis and strategy	Content performance analytics
	Audience (web and social media) analysis tools
Audience analysis	Web personalization and testing tools
	Content performance tools
Content creation	Automated video creation tools
	Graphics tools for image, GIF and video creation
	Content calendars and scheduling tools
Hub creation	Interactive hub development
Social media management	Social media management and performance
	Social listening tools
Content management	Digital asset management systems
	Content marketing platforms

It can be too easy to get carried away with IT-based analysis alone but it's also important to analyse and engage with the softer side and outcomes of your brand journalism and storytelling, and how those stories resonate with the real people you are trying to connect with. Here's Mark Schaefer's view from our interview on data and its power in marketing – what we should and shouldn't take note of:

> I think the biggest problem that companies have right now is that they're obsessed with technology. Technology has become the enemy of great marketing, not because technology is evil or bad, it's because it's so good. It's so easy. It's so inexpensive. It's so intoxicating. And so we keep adding to our MarTech stack, we keep investing even though the research shows 80 per cent of CMOs don't even understand the technology that they already have.
>
> We've got our heads in dashboards, we're trying to look for the 'marketing easy' button that just doesn't exist anymore. We need to get our heads out of the dashboards and get off the technology and get back to our customers to create real human relationships, to get out there and talk to our customers, listen to our customers. We're just too really intoxicated with technology and the key to building trust is to create really human-centred marketing, and that starts with connecting with the needs of your customers and building emotion with your customers.[3]

The only certainty in digital marketing today is change, and the range of technology available to marketers across the brand journalism journey is only going to get broader. Whatever you choose to support your planning, storytelling and distribution, ensure this is an iterative process, with a test-and-learn approach at its heart.

Notes

1   Altimeter (nd) The 2018 State of Digital Content, *Prophet*. Available from: https://insights.prophet.com/2018-state-of-digital-content (archived at https://perma.cc/329P-MLEV)
2   Schantin, D (2018) 4 characteristics of newsroom employees ready for digital transformation, *INMA*, 18 July. Available from: https://www.inma.org/blogs/media-leaders/post.cfm/4-characteristics-of-newsroom-employees-ready-for-digital-transformation (archived at https://perma.cc/N6XL-M5GW)
3   Schaefer, M (2019) Interview with Gay Flashman, May 2019

INDEX